E as in Echo

E as in Echo

A life from the bush to Bay Street

David Wheeler

gatekeeper press™

Columbus, Ohio

E as in Echo: A life from the bush to Bay Street

Published by Gatekeeper Press
2167 Stringtown Rd, Suite 109
Columbus, OH 43123-2989
www.GatekeeperPress.com

The cover design, interior formatting, typesetting, and editorial work for this book are entirely the product of the author. Gatekeeper Press did not participate in and is not responsible for any aspect of these elements.

Library of Congress Control Number: 2021937227

ISBN (hardcover): 9781662913051

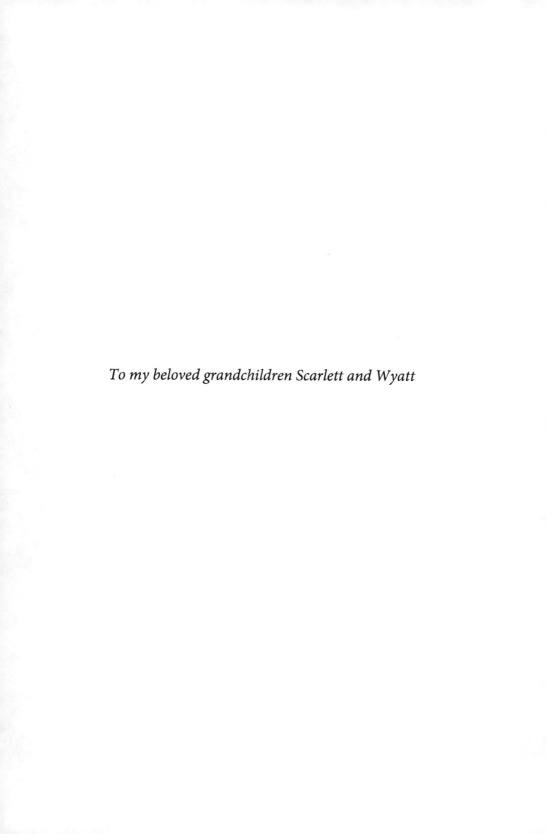

To my beloved grandchildren Scarlett and Wyatt

CONTENTS

CAROL

Up from the subway running, leaving the TTC Saint Patrick Station behind she walked up University Avenue, a cold wind off the lake at her back. Through the canyon of steel and glass towers that make up Toronto's skyline, the new overpowering the old stone buildings. Turning off at Elm Street the front entry to Sick Kids Hospital took her in along with the crowd. Striding with confidence to the reception desk she announced her business:

"Good morning, I have an appointment with Mr. Stevens. My name is Carol Ethier".

All three heads behind the desk turned at once with the announcement. The receptionist replied "one moment please" while she reached for the phone. The Sick Kids Hospital CEO had advised Carol that he would alert the staff. His Executive Assistant had called ahead and directed reception to be ready for this name.

Carol looked away and her mind went to another place.

"How is it that I have gotten here?" Her mind's voice said while her thoughts drifted hundreds of miles north.

1

What is it about that moment when our machines defy us, the horror, and the tragedy that they wreak? The stage goes completely silent, no voices can be heard. An open mouth holds back a scream. We witness the destruction of a life in terror and time stands still.

The touch on an arm brought her back. "Ms. Ethier" she heard. "Please use elevator four to the twelfth floor".

Carol's smile lit her eyes, "Thank You" and she turned away.

She thought of their first meeting. A chance encounter they had at a conference on philanthropy. She introduced herself and John Stevens replied, "I know who you are, and I have been wanting to meet you". Perhaps it wasn't a chance meeting at all. John got right to the point. "Sick Kids Hospital is mounting a $995 million dollar funding initiative and we want you to steer it". Carol was stunned but poised. John continued, "Your reputation in Toronto is impeccable and your work in fundraising is above excellent." Carol tried to demure.

"I am authorized to offer you a substantial salary, complete control for hiring and managing staff, outfitting offices, whatever you need".

Carol steadied herself. "I am working you know." She said.

"Yes, would you like for me to talk to Ben?" John offered.

Hearing the name of the Board Chairman at the Foundation where Carol was working made her pause. She thought of the promise that she had made to her employers.

"Can I think about this and get back to you?" Carol asked.

John said that he would like an answer now, but he understood. He gave Carol his card and asked, "can we meet tomorrow?".

"Yes," Carol replied, "8:30 tomorrow evening" she said.

"That late?" John asked.

"I work late," said Carol.

John knew about Carol's reputation for dedication and diligence, he smiled and made the date.

When they met the next day John ordered a cocktail, Carol decaf tea. "I'll be in bed in an hour" explained Carol.

The offer was laid out in detail. More salary and control than any position that Carol had ever achieved. She was thrilled but wary.

From her beginnings in business as a shop owner in Blind River, Ontario she had always proven herself up to any task, but this was extraordinary. That familiar self-doubt was creeping in.

She thought, "I'm just a farm girl from nowhere in North Ontario…Kynoch!"

It made her think of her Mother, Edna Tapp, and quiet strength.

The twelfth floor doors slid open to reveal the executive offices to Sick Children's Hospital Toronto, no opulence, just efficiency. John's executive assistant Kay was there waiting with a genuine huge smile to greet her and John standing just behind. Carol at once felt welcomed and wanted. Coffee was offered and declined.

"Please join us in the conference room and we'll get started." Kay said.

Carol was no newcomer to this business of fundraising. After her success at creating and running five different businesses in Blind River she sold all five at just the right time. Retired as a young wife and mother Carol was content in her life, for a short time. The need to prosper and achieve never left her.

There was an offer from a family run furniture store in sales that she took with no salary. When time past and Carol's commissions were increasing, the company's owner had to call her in. It seems that most of the sales were all totaling on Carol's ledger and there was not enough money for the family members to be made. Carol would have to be let go.

The local hospital in that remote north Ontario locale was in serious need of replacement and modernization. A million dollars was needed for this impossible endeavor to match a government grant for the same amount. They came to Carol to lead this fundraising effort and she gladly took on the challenge.

Keep in mind where this was all taking place. The northern shore of Lake Huron is a desolate place of small towns dependent on an economy of farming the rocky Canadian Shield, mining for nickel and uranium and not much else. The general response she got when asking for a donation was "let the government take care of it".

Carol dug in and went to work. Seemingly from nowhere she met their goal and exceeded a million dollars raised in eleven months. She learned how to determine what a donor can afford and asking for it, expecting it. She never forgot to show appreciation for it.

This was the key learning that drove her successful strategy from then on. The lesson became her method throughout her career.

John and Kay at Sick Kids knew a winner when they saw one and they weren't about to let Carol get away. There's a lot of pressure set when you raise the bar to almost a billion dollar fundraising. Carol's goal was to exceed that amount. She started work for the Sick Kids Hospital two weeks later.

GARNET

The memory of a six year old can be vague and uncertain. Carol's memory of that day is vivid and startling.

Garnet Tapp knew the workings of his tractor better than anyone. He knew it as well as he knew his team of Clydesdale horses. Where to touch Dan to make the team go. How to pull Sadie to make Dan stop. He knew that machine as well as he knew his wife, Edna. It was the lifeblood of his farm, made everything happen, made everything work.

That is why the tragedy of that instant is the mystery of what made Carol strong.

That Massey-Ferguson exploded in a fireball that consumed Garnet. His machine, the extension of his hands, arms, back and legs had failed him. It attacked him with a fury of fire that threw him, burned him, and killed him.

Garnet was a lean sinewy man. Tougher than the hide of any of the moose he killed to feed his family. But he was done for. Edna and Aunt Vera wrapped him in a blanket and loaded him into the Chevy for a thirty mile drive for help. It didn't matter when the headlight fell out again. No time to stop. When the car

7

ran out of gas halfway to Thessalon it stopped right where a man sat with fuel. He threw in the gas and yelled GO! Garnet lived for 21 hours.

Carol was back at the house with her baby brother and older sister. Six years old and she heard her Uncle Alvin tell the neighbor "Garnets burned". But she saw it all. Just a little girl, she saw the flash. She experienced that moment of horror. That time when no sound can be heard, the open mouth can't scream.

This is the instant in one's life that can transform a person to greatness or tear them apart to failure. When Carol looked around, she saw a farm that needs working, cows to drive and milk, chickens to feed and kill for food, pigs to tend, slaughter, a baby boy, and a sick sister. Who would it be but Carol to do all this? Carol, with the quiet strength from her mother, Edna, subconsciously chose greatness.

Garnet was a hard on the children. The product of his farming roots in the glacial rock of North Ontario. Some would say abusive, physically. It was what was required in that environment. Toughness was required to survive here. But his brothers and sisters said that he was lighthearted, fun, and playful with pranks. An early photo shows him astride a short horned heifer, big laugh on his face. His eyes were lit up just like Carol's do when she smiles. One memory Carol has of her Dad was when Edna would dress up the kids for the frequent trips to church. Garnet wasn't going.

"Why does daddy get to go fishing and I can't?" Carol would plead.

"It is God's will" said Edna again. Carol heard that phrase often from Mother.

The funeral was a blurred memory for Carol. The closed coffin in the living room. Family and friends filing in and out of the house. The children were not allowed in the room. There was no talk about the death to them. No chance to say goodbye. Garnet died a young man.

Edna was a widow now at age thirty-two with two little girls and a baby boy to raise. She had to find work to feed them, and she did. Aunt Maggie and Uncle Howard ran a store with a diner. She'd work there. Grandma Reed came to live with them, but her heart was weak and failing. She could watch the kids but not much else. There was the team of Clydesdales, Dan, and Sadie. There were sixteen cows, six pigs, chickens all wanting to be fed morning and night. The crop in the fields to take in for winter survival. Many Aunts, Uncles and cousins were close by. Neighboring farms supplied some help, but they had their own survival to tend. Carol was out there, as she says: "in the middle of nowhere". Childhood was over.

Carol's sister suffered from seizures on a regular basis. They didn't know then what it was and of course there wasn't any medicine. It fell to Carol to farm that land. It fell to Carol to feed those children. Edna was amazingly strong and resilient, but she could not do it alone. It fell to Carol. She promised herself to help their mother, to not complain and never cry. If she had to relieve that stress it was out in the bush. Don't show mum that you're scared or sad. Can't let brother or sister catch on. Live with quiet strength as Edna did and never resent it.

Every morning after the milking by hand she would let the cows out to pasture. Every evening she would take turns with the horses to bring the cows in for milking again. Climbing the ladder, she could call out Dan one day and ride out bareback. The next day it was Sadie's turn. The horses were huge and gentle. Carol was like a speck on their backs. They knew to move to the ladder so that Carol could dismount. If a cow isn't milked it dies and we will not have a dead cow. Those animals were Carol's friends and loved ones. She loved the cows and couldn't hurt them as she pulled the bags for milk and they kicked her off the stool.

She loved the pigs and was joyful for their many litters. It was always a runt of the litter that she favored. Move one of the fat little ones out of the way and hook the runt up to suckle. Uncle Ed would wonder how that little runt was growing, why didn't it die off. Carol kept the smile to herself. Of course, they would all have to die when they were grown. Carol would help Uncle with the slaughter. She knew that they had to die and give up their bodies for survival. It is the way of the farm.

She did not love the chickens. The beaks would peck at her as she took their eggs. An aversion to birds exists to this day. It didn't hurt her as much when a chicken had to go. A small girl with a large hatchet to chop off its head. It made her sad to hear a pig squeal its last. With the chickens it was one less head with its angry eyes to stab at her cold hands. Sometimes older sister Colleen was well enough to help. Brother Blaine was five years younger and needed to be watched closely. Mother, with quiet strength, was always the force that ran the farm. Carol was determined to draw from that and help her.

Carol did have a helper early on. Laddie was the collie dog that Garnet had trained for farm work. He was a barn dog and never came into the house further than the entry where he was fed. Despite Carol trying he would not set a paw beyond the doorframe and into the kitchen. He was that well trained. After Garnet was killed Laddie seemed to take on a more protective role. When Carol would take the horse out to collect the cows in the evening Laddie walked alongside. If a cow lagged behind, he would be there to nip at its heels and hurry it along. He stood sentry as they cows filed into the barn and then followed the last one in. After cow duty in the morning Laddie would be there in the yard watching over the chickens and children. Not letting any of them stray too far. If Carol needed to get away in trying times she would walk into the bush with Laddie. They would sit close while Carol had a cry and Laddie gave love.

Carol loved Laddie more than all of her animals. He would sit still beside her and was content with her long tight hugs around his neck. Laddie was happy to take time off from his job to play with her in the yard. The dirt road that ran in front of the farm didn't see much traffic, but an occasional car or truck would fly by. Laddie was trained not to go near the road and to keep the kids and animals away too.

One warm fall day soon after Garnet's death Carol was in the yard maybe too close to the road and Laddie was barking as a car sped toward the farm. He had never chased after a car before, but something must have sensed danger in him this time. He went at the car as if to herd it away from the kids. The impact killed him instantly. The car never slowed, and Carol was left alone in the trailing dust by the side of the road, grieving the loss of another loved one. She pulled him back into the yard with arms around his neck as his good soul left him. She stayed with him sobbing for hours until mother came home from her job and found them there in the yard. Carol pulled herself together quickly and showed strength to her mother as she told her about what happened. They gave Laddie an honored grave near the kitchen door.

Imagine all of this to deal with as a young girl and still there was school. When the morning chores were done on the farm, they next walked miles to school. Kynoch was the name they gave the area near the farm that Garnet and the Tapp family had settled on. It was little more than a mud road but there was a one room schoolhouse for all grades. Heated with a wood stove, and cold still Carol remembers those freezing days and her feet always being cold.

The Tapp girls would line their pants with cardboard because the neighbors' dogs would attack and tear at them as they walked to school. Carol would always enjoy getting away to school or church simply as an escape from the boredom of the farm. There was no television or radio there. Not even a book or magazine, only the never ending work.

After Garnet was killed Carol came to the realization that she had to emulate her Mother. Drawing on the same quiet strength as Edna, she persevered.

DOUGLAS

There were vegetables growing in between the rocks that were anchored in the earth outside of their house in Kynoch. Edna would tend them when she could, but Carol would pamper them, especially the corn and tomatoes. In the fall before a frost Carol would cover them and dream about how good they would be once they ripened. "if we can pick them just before the freeze comes we'll have a fine crop" Carol said to Mum. The hard freeze always comes early to Kynoch and tomatoes froze on the vine. Corn didn't get a chance to ripen. Growing seemed to be a senseless exercise. They ate them anyway.

It was a beautiful warm spring day and a couple of years since Garnet had died. Carol and her Mum had decided that they would clear a patch of land overgrown with tall grass and weeds. The patch was between the house and the barn and had fewer rocks and decent soil. Carol's job was to lay out the boundaries with stones. The spot got good sunlight and promised a better chance for the crop to thrive. Edna spilled out some gasoline from a can and struck a match to it.

"Let it smolder for a bit more, then we can rake it up and turn the earth" said Edna. Carol thought about picking out the small boulders and making a ring around their garden.

Sister was lying down in the house after a spell. Grandma was in her rocker knitting with eyes moving back and forth to baby brother on the floor. She had just put soup on the stove for dinner.

Late afternoon and a cold wind from the North signaled a change in the weather. With increasing force, the wind swept up the little smoldering grass fire into a blaze. Edna tossed the rake aside and yelled to Carol "go inside and start pumping the water" Carol sprang. "tell Grandma to keep filling pots and you bring them out here." Edna, always in her housedress tore off the apron, tossed it down on the fire and started stamping it out.

Carol arrived with the first bucket and threw water at the fire. Before turning to sprint back she could see the fire moving fast toward the barn. Fear rose from her toes to her throat and choked her. Terrified that her friends in the barn, horses, cows, pigs are in danger. How many times back to the kitchen for water, run out and throw it at the fire. It must have been a hundred trips.

Edna and Carol beat down the last of the flames with rags and blankets. The fire had burned right up to the barn and scorched the wall. They got it stopped, coughing up smoke they were exhausted. Carol could not stop the fear and terror. Fire again had come to threaten their lives. "what could we do if we lost the barn" Carol thought. "If my dear animals were killed, how could we make it".

The memory from that day came back over and over. A warm fire in the fireplace can't be enjoyed. Carol won't see movies or watch a show that involves fire. Now two major events in her early years that involve the terror of fire have forged that fear in her. You can't live without fire on the farm and in the northern region of Ontario, but Carol is always careful.

The campaign for Sick Kids Hospital was in full swing. Carol had spent the first weeks acquiring space within the building. Furnishings and decor were picked out with an eye on budget but reflected on Carol's fine taste. She put the most attention into the hiring of staff. Her interviews focused on a candidate's ability to research and their knowledge of Canada's philanthropic community. All of the pieces were in place and the work began.

Not only did the hospital need it but Carol's drive and ambition required it. She needed to make a big deal. They had to acquire a major donation from a prominent donor.

Carol paced while she waited at the main entrance. Their arrival time had passed 30 minutes ago. "should I go back to the office and call?" she wondered. "Are they even coming?" she worried.

The couple arrived by limousine right at the front door. Carol went out to meet them and was promptly brushed back as the driver sprinted to get the rear door. Emerging first was the eldest son of an ancient Toronto family. They had built their fortune over centuries of manufacturing in Canada and beyond. He was still a CEO and board member of numerous firms. He turned for the hand of his wife helping her from the car. She is tall and classically beautiful, and her well-tailored fur not concealing a slim figure. One of the leading members of Toronto's society, she is well respected for her constant interest in charity.

"Good morning and welcome back to Sick Kids" Carol interjected.

"Good morning" she replied "and we are so sorry to be late. The traffic on Bloor Street was horrible" Carol imagined their stately home in Rosedale.

Her husband extended his right hand to greet Carol. "We regret keeping you waiting, can we get started?" He seemed nervous.

Carol knew that this couple were familiar to the hospital, they had been most generous to the cause in the past but never to this extent. Carol had begun correspondence with a letter. A call to the woman's secretary confirmed an appointment, at their home in Rosedale soon after that, Carol had asked them for two million dollars.

There was no pause from the couple, no raised eyebrows. These were poised and positioned people.

"We would like to see what progress is being made at the hospital" the wife replied.

"In particular I would like to tour the burn unit" he said. "I have a personal interest".

Carol's history with fire made the burn unit at Sick Kids unpleasant and uneasy for her.

"Wonderful" Carol beamed "I will arrange the tour and schedule with your secretary."

The work that went into getting these donors through the door was arduous and now the day has arrived.

As they walked across the lobby floor towards the elevators Carol kept up a light conversation. Mentioning people, they knew at the hospital, a prominent surgeon.

"Hey gorgeous"! Carol heard the high pitched voice croaking from behind her.

"Hey gorgeous"! She turned expecting to see an older man calling, she ignored it.

The wheelchair rolled by and blocked their path. "I'm talking to you gorgeous" He seemed to be about four years old. A cancer patient with very thin hair, iv's dripping into ports, voice rough from treatments. Strong arms and hands, he handled the wheelchair well.

"I'm sorry" Carol replied bending a knee "I didn't realize that you were talking to me". Carol looked up at the couple smiling down at them and back to the boy. "How about if we meet later in the cafeteria, I'll buy you a milk. Who is your nurse?"

"It's a deal. I'm on the third floor, oncology" said the boy and he wheeled past them and out into the lobby.

The tour continued on to the burn unit. Carol, prepared as always, answered many of their questions and concerns. As uncomfortable as she was, she didn't show it. They visited the research facility that was to be the focus of this campaign. Introductions were made to administrators who could expand on the details necessary for the fundraising. These intelligent and well connected donors had to be impressed with the level of expertise brought to bear that day. At the end of the tour, they sat in a conference room and a phone was offered to call for the couple's car. Carol accompanied them to the door shaking hands and thanking them for their time.

"We will be in touch with you very shortly Carol" The woman promised. Carol smiled warmly. She knew that a pledge would be forthcoming.

Later that day close to dinner time Carol went down to oncology. She approached the desk nurse and described her earlier encounter with the boy in the lobby: "I know just who you mean, Douglas". She gave Carol the room number and pointed down the hall. There was Douglas in his chair as if waiting for their date. "Let's go!" He said rolling his chair to the elevators, Carol followed.

At the cafeteria she took a tray and two milks, paid, and joined Douglas at a table. He talked and talked as if to spill out his entire short life story in minutes. Carol was tired from a long day but kept up the conversation with grace and compassion. In the end Douglas asked, "Can we have another date tomorrow?"

"If I can manage it, I'll be here" Carol promised.

She didn't make it the next day, but Carol met with Douglas over a shared carton milk many more times over the next few weeks. One day he said: "You know, they don't like me to have chocolate milk, but as a treat, that's what I like" She thought he was so mature, he had been through so much.

The cheque for the two million dollar gift came along with a personal letter from the wife of the couple donors. She explained that a discussion had ensued with a group of charitable associates of the couple. Names and phone numbers of contacts were given to Carol.

Four weeks of hard work and research went into the planning of a meeting with these contacts. The group of six represented the most charitable of five wealthy families in Toronto. They were assembled one morning in the lobby at Sick Kids. The asking was to be for eight million dollars.

The lobby at Sick Kids is a bustling place. Everywhere you look there are children, some well, most not. Families are gathered together. Moms and dads, grandparents visiting from all parts of the province and beyond. They come to the lobby because it's a warm place and brightly lit with large windows facing all directions. Of course, it's an escape for a short time from the wards and the clinics that are the reality of their struggle with illness.

Carol was reviewing the outline of the scheduled tour that was about to take place. They were to visit a few different floors and a discussion with the cancer researchers and senior administrators would follow. As she prepared to lead them to the elevators everything suddenly went black.

The group looked on stunned as a small boy in a big wheelchair moved quickly. The chair struck Carol from behind with a force that upended her. She landed square on her head on the terrazzo floor and was knocked out cold.

When she came to the group was standing around her, one knelt beside her. "That little boy in a wheelchair hit you intentionally" he said.

"Where is he?" Carol asked, but her eyes were clearing now, and she saw Douglas sitting by the windows crying.

Pulling herself together Carol got to her feet. "I'll be just a minute" she told them, and she walked shakily over to Douglas.

"Douglas, I'll see you at five o'clock in the cafeteria, we'll chat."

"Are you mad at me?" he gulped; the tears were streaming down his face. "I'm not mad at you but we'll talk" she replied.

The tour continued. Carol fought through the pain in her head not to mention the fuzziness she felt. She led another outstanding presentation describing the needs required and the good work to be done after the success of this fundraising. The group responded by pledging to contribute the eight million dollars.

Five o'clock came and Carol met Douglas in the cafeteria. He was crying again.

"Why did you do that?" Carol asked, trying very hard to show no anger.

"Because you didn't pay any attention to me" was Douglas's answer.

Her voice softened. "I'm sorry, I didn't see you." Carol explained what she had been working on that morning. "I'm hoping to get eight million dollars from those nice people for all you kids".

Douglas was not consoled; "Well, I won't be alive to use it anyway"

He died less than two weeks later.

Carol went to the visitation for Douglas. It was in a small town east of Toronto, of course she didn't know anyone there. She found his parents and said: "I knew Douglas at the hospital" and offered her sympathies.

Turning to leave she heard "Wait a minute, are you Carol?" Douglas' mother looked happy.

"Yes, I'm Carol". "I got to know Douglas quite well at Sick Kids".

"He always told us that he was going to marry you"

It truly is a labor of love to work for these kids. Whenever one of the staff in the Development Department would come in grumpy, if there was a complaint because the demands seemed too great, Carol would say: "Go for a walk in the lobby and you'll feel a lot better when you come back."

KYNOCH

Thomas Tapp left Victorian England in the bowels of a steamship bound for Canada. Being a stowaway then was not necessarily a criminal act. A place on board could be bought or bartered for with the crew. Thomas was a runaway with his little brother in tow from the orphanage. Imagine Oliver Twist, Thomas was six years old. He and the little brother made their way onto this ship because they had no choice, no hope to survive in industrializing England. Canada offered hope and opportunity. How does one realize that at six years old? It comes from hunger.

Thomas's little brother died on that passage. The boiler tenders wrapped his little body in a wool blanket and carried it up to the rail. Thomas followed along up the ladders into the foggy cold of the North Atlantic. A few strange words were said over the body before the men pushed it over the edge and it was gone from sight. He had looked after him since their parents had died of disease that was rampant then in Great Britain. Throughout the horror that was the orphanage he kept the little boy alive with the meager food they were given. Everything that he knew and loved was now gone and Thomas was at that juncture of failure or greatness. At six years old, devastated by death, Thomas moved on.

The ship came into sight of land in the new world and Thomas had no idea, he stayed below. It sailed down the throat of the Saint Lawrence, never stopping at Quebec or Montreal. Passing Kingston and now entering into Lake Ontario they were bound for Toronto. Thomas was put off the ship there with nothing but his wits. What caused Thomas to keep moving is unknown, but he moved on. It must have been that same innate grit and determination that showed itself in his granddaughter Carol two generations later.

Canada offered refuge to the displaced migrants from the British Empire. Thousands arrived during this time of famine and disease from Ireland, Wales, Scotland, and England. Their new home meant survival and hope. Thomas Tapp found a home at one of the many orphanages that operated in the province. From an early age the children were taught trades that would be of benefit to the growing new country. Thomas was moved to a rural location to the West.

His trade was to become farming and all of the skills required for self-sufficiency. His long days of hard work were a multiple of tasks. As he grew to a young man, he learned the tending of animals. He was taught the growing, harvesting and storage of their feed. The production of milk, butter, and cheese. The slaughter for meat, hide and tallow. A farmer has to know carpentry and building skills in order to operate their isolated enterprise. As Thomas grew stronger and more skilled, he mastered the machinery that ran the modern farms.

At a time somewhere around the age of fifteen the institution that ran these training homes would find employment for the young men and women. Thomas was placed with a family farm further to the West. The institution would receive compensation from the farmer for his work. Thomas would receive room and board and a very small wage. He saved what he could and looked forward to the day that he could strike out on his own. Nearing the age of eighteen his obligation to the farmer ended and Thomas was free to pursue his own life.

He found himself in the town of Owen Sound on the southern shore of Lake Huron. Times were booming at this small port city and Thomas found work. He put to use the skills that he had learned in building and machinery and began to earn a living wage. He saw the freedom from struggle that his employers earned and wanted it for himself. Thomas kept moving on.

Land was being offered off to the North as Ontario was looking to populate their territory. For a desperate man yearning for freedom the horizon he sees promises hope. Thomas boarded another ship on Lake Huron headed north. Now at twenty years old and a grown man he landed in a place called Dean Lake, nearby what is now Blind River. Again, finding work and again dreaming to be free on his own land. Small success came to him through sheer hard work. He met and married another pioneer, a refugee from Ireland who shared his desire for land. A family was started that would eventually grow to thirteen children. They pushed on further north.

The young family acquired that land thirty-six more miles from Blind River. Driving a team and wagon loaded with tools and essentials through the wilderness. The Irish immigrants that founded this place called it Kynoch after their homeland. The Tapp family had land and they set to work building a farm out of this wilderness. A house went up, a shed for the animals would become a barn. Trees were felled and stumps pulled, rock moved, and crops were planted. These strong, resilient survivors built a life from nothing that became rooted into the deep granite Canadian Shield.

As was common in those days, not all of the Tapp's thirteen children lived to grown ages. There were some that were lost in childbirth. It was a tough existence with many dangers. Those that did survive populated the area around Kynoch.

The youngest one of them, Garnet Tapp eventually bought the farm that his parents, Thomas, and Annie had built. In less than one generation that farm had become a success. It afforded the family a decent life. They grew their food and raised livestock and were well fed. Days were filled with hard work, but time could be spared for spiritual beliefs. The church and religion became important. When you have come from nothing and feel blessed to be delivered from what could have been hell, it is only natural to thank God.

Garnet married Edna Reed and soon after they bought the farm from Thomas. They worked hard to make it pay and it did. Colleen was born first; Carol followed a year later. The girls were raised in a strict manner. Edna was very religious, stoic and never affectionate. Garnet would mete out punishment as a means to training. Our modern times might label it abuse; this was a different world. There was no newspaper or magazine in the house, despite being the early fifties, radio or television didn't exist to them. The girls knew nothing of the outside world except for church. They would attend two days a week and Sundays were a day for quiet reflection. No games or play were allowed. After church, the girls just sat quietly in the house all day.

At least church and bible school were a social release for Carol, and she looked forward to it. She made friends and they could talk about what little there was to observe about that life in isolation. Carol felt that strong need for social interaction at a very young age. It only grew in intensity and is Carol's best personality trait. The early exposure to what seemed to her as loveless parents has molded Carol into an extremely loving and giving person.

Besides this, Carol's earliest memories of the farm were the animals and she always loved them as friends. Her father had trained two huge and powerful Clydesdale draft horses. When a boulder needed moving or a tree stump pulled it was always more efficient to employ the team. They worked for their feed like a family member. There was a small herd of cows for dairy. Milk not used for the house was sold as cream, butter, or cheese. Carol can recall turning the crank for hours on that butter churn. Calves born in the spring were sold and slaughtered.

Carol most loved the pigs and especially piglets, fat, fuzzy, pink, and cute. They had sheep and of course lambs born in spring also. Chickens were kept penned and protected. There were still wolves that roamed in the area. Garnet kept the wolves away and probably killed many as punishment to train the pack to stay away. Deer, moose, and other game rounded out the diet and they were hung from a beam near the barn.

Death was an early experience to Carol. It is just the way of life on a farm. Sometimes her friends the animals had to be harvested for the family's survival.

Carol's little brother was born when she was five years old, and they were all so happy.

Ten months later death came to deal a tragic blow to the Tapps. Garnet was killed.

Edna never spoke to the girls about their father again. It was as if he didn't exist except that Carol had memories. It might have been that her mother feared that remembering Garnet would trigger emotions that she couldn't afford to show.

With her father gone and mother having to work away from home, the isolation that Carol felt on the farm became overwhelming. Her grandparents Thomas and Annie Tapp had moved across the road after selling Garnet the farm. Just a couple of weeks after Garnet died Thomas passed away. Carol loved Grandma Annie so much. She was loving and affectionate unlike her mother. Annie passed away soon after Thomas and Carol felt devastated.

There was no time for mourning though. The work to save the farm had to continue. Carol saw the strength that her mother showed, and she drew from it. If she felt fear from the harsh environment around them, she couldn't show it. Any sadness that Carol felt had to be suppressed. She could not let her mother see any of it for fear of hurting her. Hiding her emotions only increased the feeling of isolation.

They heated the farmhouse with wood and Carol had to chop it, stack it, and haul it in. Bath night was once a week and the water had to be hauled up a hill from the well and into the house.

Heated on the wood stove it was poured into a tub for brother first. Sister went next and Carol was last, the water then was cold.

"Can I just have one more pot of hot water?" Carol asked her mother.

"No, you'd have to go down to the well and fetch another pail." Mother said. It was dark outside now and the walk to the well was difficult.

The winter months were brutally cold in the farmhouse in Kynoch. It was common for temperatures to reach forty below zero outside. When the girls would wake up in the morning their first move was to the stove in the kitchen. Trying to get the dying fire inside going with kindling and blowing, it would take some time to warm up just the kitchen. The pail of water in the sink had a thick layer of ice on the top. When it had thawed enough to move, they could start making a breakfast.

Edna had quiet strength and Carol would be strong for her. There would be no resentment for her situation. There would be no complaining about the work that had to done. If she needed a shoulder to cry on it would be their collie dog Laddie that lived in the barn. She had to be tough like her father. She had to become like her father to survive.

MOTHER

Aunt Margaret and Uncle Lloyd were at the house with their four kids when mother got back from the hospital. She never told us that father had died. She didn't say one word to sister and me but we heard her tell the others. I knew at that moment that my life was totally changed.

Carol was six years old and thought, "Who's going to milk the cows, feed them and clean the stalls". "Who's going to collect the eggs, kill and dress a chicken?" The answer, it was her.

Colleen and Carol sat at the back of the living room while all the people streamed by the coffin. Nobody spoke to them at all. It was like a bad dream. Finally, Aunt Rhoda took them back into a bedroom, She doesn't remember if they slept. Next day Aunt Marg and Uncle Lloyd came into the house and got on their knees in front of the coffin. They were very religious and prayed that father would be in heaven. Carol just had to get up and leave, she wasn't believing what they were saying. She went outside to cry alone.

Mother had to take a job in town after that. Aunt and Uncle had a gas station and store that had a lunch counter. It was on the

Chapleau highway, twenty miles from the farm. That took her away from home for long hours, but she had no choice. Grandma Reed came to live with them, and Carol loved her very much. She was ill with a bad heart, but she could keep an eye on the kids. Colleen was getting worse with her illnesses. Seizures were happening almost daily. Their little brother was just a baby when mother had to go to work.

"What do you do if your grandma has a heart attack?" mother would ask me?

"I give her this pill and that to drink" I would answer

"And if your sister has a seizure?"

"Make sure she doesn't hit her head on the way down or swallow her tongue"

"And your brother?"

"I won't take my eyes off him" She said. The farm was remote and had many dangers. The road in front saw cars and trucks speeding by too fast. There was the livestock and wild animals outside those doors, a creek ran behind our house.

Carol didn't think that she was poor or overworked. It never occurred to her that this was a terrible injustice for a kid to endure. She just put her head down and did it. Carol saw the strength that her mother showed when we lost father. She quietly drew on her faith and set about keeping our family alive. She learned from a very young age to pattern herself after her mother's quiet strength.

Colleen's illness came and went and got worse. She could be indifferent toward Carol. When she got angry Carol would have hide from her or try to. How could you hide when there was always too much to do? Colleen was older and much bigger and, disturbed by her illnesses, Carol seemed a nuisance to her. Grandma Reed saw what was going on and would try to intervene. Sometimes it worked, sometimes not.

Growing up in this religious home Carol's one relief from the boredom and drudgery was church and the Bible study. There were so many instances that shaped her beliefs. Later organized religions held no place in Carol's life, but strong spirituality remained. Carol had a yearning to learn from an early age. There was never anything in the home to read except for the Bible so Carol read it cover to cover, twice. There were always lots of questions in her mind. Carol would ask her mother about things that the Minister said, contradictions. Edna's answer time after time would be "Children are to be seen and not heard".

The Tapp's had an Uncle Matt that lived three or four farms away. He never went to church, but he was a lovely, kind man, Carol relates. He did things for them discreetly, but she always knew it was Uncle Matt who had done it. The Aunts and Uncles would talk badly about him saying what a terrible man he was for not going to church. Carol's thoughts were "how can you say that you are Christians and Uncle Matt is a good man doing good things for people". It's what started her thinking that often organized religion may not mean spirituality.

The year father died Carol started school. Colleen had already started the year before. They would walk the road to the little one room schoolhouse. It was a pitiful collection of worn out battered desks surrounding a potbellied stove. No more than a shack with no insulation it was never warm there. The wintertime walks to school could see minus 40 degree temperatures. Mr. Trivers would open early and get a fire going in the stove. Arriving at the school they would prop their frozen feet up near the stove and start lessons. The teacher would hand out papers to work on in their laps in pencil.

It was thirty-two kids in all grades from first to eighth grade. Carol's grade was just her and a boy. Mother heard her refer to the boy as Pudding Face and she was punished for a month. The two would compete through the whole eight years. If he got a grade of 97, she got 98. If he got a 98, she was determined to get 99 and they went back and forth. He was always teasing her and said some hurtful things. There were awful names he called her but the one that stuck most was "stupid".

On a walk home from school one day Carol swung her lunch bucket and hit him in the head. He lived about two miles before the Tapp's house. She thought: "When I get home his mother is going to call mine and I'm in trouble." Sure enough, she called.

When Carol walked into the house Mother said: "Let me see your lunch pail Carol". She showed her the side that wasn't dented in. "Let me see the other side" mum said. So, she showed her. She always knew that mother got a kick out of that. The boy's mother was always complaining about something.

"Why did you hit him" Mother asked?

"I just couldn't take it anymore" she said. "Pudding Face said that I'm stupid and that my dad is dead, and I won't amount to anything because of it". She wasn't punished for it.

Carol's teacher from first to third grade was Mr. Brown. He was a kind man, but what good teacher would go into the backwoods and board at someone's house to teach in a humble building with eight grades. He was from the city of Sault Ste. Marie about 200 miles away and was probably Carol's first crush.

The school had only two books, both from the Bobbsey Twins series. She wrote a book report on these same books every year. There was nothing at her home to offer any enlightenment. They had no radio or television and never a magazine of newspaper in the house. It's amazing but somehow Carol did learn to read and write.

She was in the second grade when Mr. Brown said to her: "Could you handle teaching grade one?" She was thrilled and said that she could. Being so bored with all that life in this remote Northern area did not have to offer. Carol's yearning for something more, more knowledge, more opportunity had to show through to this teacher. She knew nothing about what was out in the world but always held out hope that there was more. Mr. Brown must have seen that there was a desire for a better life in Carol.

These years went by in a blur of school time and then home to the chores on the farm. As the boys in school grew older into the sixth or seventh grade many would quit to become farmers.

Every year the school would put on a Christmas concert. There were small plays and songs sung in the Kynoch Hall across from the school. To Carol it was the event of the year because they would practice in the big town hall. She loved to act and would always have a part in the plays. The students all sang in the choir. Everyone in the community came and it was such a big memory for her. Years later she was working in Sault Ste. Marie and lived with Aunt Blanche and Uncle Herb. They all drove back to Kynoch for the Christmas concert and Carol walked into that big hall and thought: "What happened, it shrunk!". Of course, it hadn't but after being away in the city it just seemed so different.

Kynoch Hall was the place for every wedding reception or party in the community. Carol has happy memories there of music and friends and dancing. She loves dancing and music ever since those days.

The livestock was being sold off or slaughtered for food now and Carol was in the thick of it. Uncles would come by and pigs were killed in the barn. A long knife to the throat and they squealed and shrieked as the blood flowed to the ground and they died. Carol's memories of this are vivid and strangely matter of fact. Again, she knew no different life, she imagined that all kids must know this.

Saturday night was bath night. They had a big round galvanized tub and mother would fill it with pots of hot water off the wood burning stove. She would bathe Blaine first, then it was sister's turn. Carol was always last, and the water would be cold by then. She would beg mother: "Can I just have one more pot of hot water"?

"No" She said: " You'll have to go down the hill and get another pail if you want that".

It was dark by then and a hard steep climb back up the hill. Carol was always cold as a child.

Towards the end of every month the food would run short in the fridge. They'd go down in the root cellar and dig out some rotting potatoes and carrots or whatever they could find to eat. If it were summertime Carol could go to the creek and catch fish for dinner. Sometimes there was moose meat or venison left in the freezer.

But the end of the month meant a trip to town in Mum's car for groceries. She received a "Mother's allowance" from the federal government, $75.00 a month. It was the great big deal of Carol's life then. Paved roads and sidewalks, it seemed like a city but Thessalon is just a small town. Cousins had given the girls some car coats to wear. Just stiff, straight fabrics with button up fronts. The floorboards in that car were rusted out and they would tape cardboard down but the dust from those dirt roads still poured in. Once in town the coats would come off and their clothes were clean, but faces were dirty.

It was usually after dark when they headed back on the road to Kynoch. Traveling down the bumpy dirt roads the headlights shook crazily and then went black. The light had fallen out of the frame. "Carol, tape the light back in" Mum said. She'd get the tape and get out and fix it. A little further down the road the other headlight would come loose. Get out again and tape that one in.

On one of these trips the car hit an owl and it was stuck down in front. Mum stopped and from the front seat she said: "Carol, go move that bird". Carol got out and the owl was laying in the road, still alive but suffering. She had to grab it by that scrawny claw and drag it to the side. I wanted to kill it, but the beak was terrifying to me. She felt terrible about it.

Mother stayed on that farm for over fifteen years and raised the three children, a widow, isolated and alone, a woman in the prime of her life. Carol had so much admiration for her. After the father was killed, she observed her strength, her quiet strength. She just plowed ahead and got through all the challenges.

Mother never told them anything about their father. What Carol was able to learn about him came from her Aunt Blanche, his sister. They had been very close. She was like a second mother to Carol and offered hugs and affection. Carols mother never expressed emotion, never said: "I love you". No hugs or kisses it was "goodnight, go to bed".

"I only saw my mother cry once throughout these times and I never wanted to see it again." Carol related to me. "That's what drove me to do all that I could for her."

Carol had to be as strong as Mum was. Mother didn't allow her to cry as a child, or maybe she didn't allow herself. If mother saw tears, she would send Carol out into the bush.

"I realize now that if I started to cry then Mum might cry and then everything would fall apart." Carol says. "I give mother full credit for the grit I have today. I was taught quiet strength."

ANNE

This story happens some years later. Carol had been working in management for different foundations after moving from the North to Oshawa then on to Toronto. She was new to the city and just beginning to feel comfortable in her role and location.

Opening the door into the offices Carol was just returning from a board meeting. She had been working in the fundraising business for some years now. This new position as CEO of the foundation was a step up that Carol navigated with ease because of hard work. That morning the call arrived at the reception desk handled by her assistant. As Carol walked past the desk, she overheard Gina.

"No, we do not pick up donations" Gina spoke into the phone.

"Wait a second" Carol commanded. "Send that call to my office"

Gina's eyes dropped and her head turned as she softened her voice.

"Please hold just a moment for Ms. Ethier". The receiver went back on its cradle with a bang. "Line two" was all that was said.

Carol entered her office and shut the door. Swinging her brief case into place at the corner of her desk she sat and reached for the phone.

"Good afternoon this is Carol, how may we help you?"

The soft, quavering voice she heard was surprising. Obviously, a woman of some age but the message was quite clear.

"Hello, my name is Anne Semple and I wish to make a large donation to your charity. I don't trust the Canada Post and I would like someone to come to my home".

"Of course, I would be glad to do that for you". "Give me your address please" Carol said. She had written Anne's name on the pad in front of her. Underneath she filled in the address.

"I live at 1022 Currie Street in Glencoe" Anne said.

"Can you spell Glencoe for me" Carol asked.

"It's G-L-E-N-C-O-E" came the reply.

"Hold just a minute please while I look that up". Carol put the phone down on her desk.

At first Carol thought this was a suburb in Toronto that she hadn't heard of. She opened a drawer and pulled out the map book. Turning to the index for Metro Toronto, there was no Glencoe. The larger index page for Ontario showed a town on page thirty-three. Carol wrote down the coordinates and turned the pages. Her finger traced a line to a spot west of Toronto. It must be a two or three hour trip by car from the office.

Having second thoughts now Carol paused then picked up the call. She spoke: "Well, that's some distance from here but maybe I could come out on the weekend".

She had grown up caring for her maternal grandmother from an early age. Her father's parents lived close, and she always had a very loving, caring relationship with her grandparents. Carol had more interaction with the elderly rather than children back in Kynoch. The sweet sound of Anne's voice had something that made Carol want to meet her. Her instincts told her that there was something there that she had to discover.

Gifts to the foundation came in many different forms and none of them considered to be strange. Carol researched Anne's address and Currie Street fell within a short walk from the Via Rail station in Glencoe, a plan was made. She told Anne that it would be her pleasure to meet with her on the following Saturday at noon. Glencoe is a two and a half hour trip from Union Station in Toronto. She would take the laptop and work to fill the hours on the trip there and back.

That Saturday Carol left her apartment for Union Station at eight to catch the Via Rail train. One quick stop for coffee and a ticket and she was on her way out to Glencoe. Deep into concentration on the work she had brought along, Carol gave no thought as to what may happen on her visit with Anne.

The announcement for Glencoe Station stirred Carol from her work and she set about putting her briefcase in order for the walk ahead. As is customary the train was perfectly timed so that Carol was leaving the station at eleven-forty, right on time. Turning right on McRae Street she found Anne's house across from a pretty little park. Carol stood on the sidewalk taking in the scene. Anne's house was lovely once. Two story with large front windows now tightly covered in drapery. The paint was peeling, a dull powdery gray. Gardens that looked like they had been tended years ago were now choked with weeds.

Carol climbed the four steps, crossed the porch, and turned the old crank doorbell on the middle of the door. Hearing the loud clang of the bell she took a step back. Seconds past and she turned the crank again. After about a minute from the first bell the inner door opened, and Anne stepped to the outer door. Opening the door as she welcomed Carol into her home, Anne was indeed very old, but her mind was sharp.

"Please do come in. I have the table set for lunch" Anne said

"Thank you so much" Carol replied, "That would be nice".

Carol followed Anne from the foyer through the front room and into the dining room. All of Anne's furniture was quite old and worn but was obviously lovely at one time. Dust covered most surfaces including the dining room table, not set. Anne directed Carol into the kitchen to the rear of the house.

"We'll dine here" Anne said. "This is where I spend most of my time" She switched off a black and white television that was playing a snowy image of CHCH news on the counter.

They sat at the table with small sandwiches that Anne had prepared on white bread with a thin slice of meat. There was tea that Anne poured from a china pot and plain cookies for dessert. They talked about small things, the trip out, weather, government. Anne drew out a little bit about Carol's family, not much.

"What can the Foundation do for you Anne?" Carol said finally, getting down to business. She told Anne that she intended to meet the three o'clock train back to Toronto.

Anne stood and walked toward a cupboard. "I have a check written here for you and I want you to know how much the foundation means to me" Anne said.

Carol made a quick glance down at the check and saw a number that surprised her. She didn't want to look at it again and folded it into a pocket. Looking up she thanked Anne so much for her kind gift and explained that she would really have to be on her way home. Goodbyes were made and Anne walked with Carol out to the front door. Carol's ears were burning as she turned onto Currie Street and walked towards the station. "had she really done this?" she heard herself asking.

When Carol got to the station, she bought her ticket and still had time to wait. She sat with her briefcase at her feet her mind racing. Reaching into her pocket she pulled out the check and unfolded it. Fifteen dollars, fifteen dollars! She came two and a half hours out here to this little town for a check that was less than the cost of the train ride. The idea that she would tell anyone about this trip was out of the question. At least she was able to get some work done in the solitude of the train ride.

It was ten days later when the intercom buzzed at Carol's desk. "yes?" she asked.

"Anne Semple is on the line" came the reply.

"Thank you" Carol replied. She took a moment to gather her thoughts. She liked the sweet old lady and felt the usual fondness for the elderly that she always had. It was impossible for Carol to be anything but gracious to Anne. And again, that intuition of hers told her that there was something about Anne that Carol just had to know.

"Good morning Anne, how have you been" Carol started.

Anne proceeded to tell Carol about her condition. The trip to the doctor in a taxi provided by the senior center. A new medication that gave her headaches. All in all, she was doing well.

43

"That's nice to hear Anne, I do have to get some work done now. Is there something that I can do before we say goodbye?" Carol asked.

Anne said in her soft weak voice. "Yes, I have another check for you. It's bigger than the last one" "Could you come again for a visit and lunch with me?" Anne pleaded.

"Of course," Carol answered without a second pause. " I'm busy Saturday but I could come on Sunday, same time"

"That would be wonderful" Anne said. She sounded so happy to have a new friend.

The same trip was repeated on that Sunday. Again, Carol took work along on the train and paid for the ticket with her own funds. They talked and talked. Anne asked all about Carol's family. Carol related about her life before she came to Toronto. Her husband was still in Blind River, so far away. Her daughter was now living with her and in university. Anne managed to get more information out of her than she wanted to reveal. The fact that Carol had to work very hard to support their family. Small parts about what she had endured growing up on the farm in Kynoch.

Carol made motions of her intention to catch the train back to Toronto and Anne produced the check from the cupboard. Carol didn't even look at it as she opened her case and slid it in. She thanked Anne very much for her gift and they made their goodbyes.

The train was on time and Carol walked into the station and stepped right on. As she took her seat and raised the brief case onto her lap, she thought for some time about the pleasant conversation they had. It was a calming visit in a turbulent time for Carol. Her husband had promised to follow her to Toronto from Blind River, hundreds of miles away. He hadn't kept that promise and they had grown farther and farther apart. Her daughter was foremost in her mind.

She glanced at Anne's check, twenty-five dollars. Carol smiled warmly and put the check away. The amount didn't matter at all.

The next call from Anne came exactly ten days later. Again, a check was promised, bigger than the last. The same trip was made, and the conversation was better than the last. Carol was able to learn more about Anne's life and it was remarkable that it was so ordinary. Just a housewife in a small Ontario town, her husband had passed years ago. The third check was bigger as promised, fifty dollars.

This same scenario was to repeat itself four more times over the next few months. Anne would call and invite Carol for a visit. And a check was offered, bigger than the last. The fourth check was a hundred dollars. The fifth check called for two hundred and Carol noticed that the handwriting was becoming weaker and shakier. They were becoming close on these visits and the conversation was soothing for Carol. She was truly enjoying her visits with Anne. The sixth check that Anne wrote was for three hundred and twenty-two dollars. It was an odd number and Carol noticed that Anne was getting tired before the end of the visit.

On the seventh visit Carol insisted on bringing the lunch and Anne finally relented. Carol couldn't help but notice that Anne's complexion had become most gray and pale. They ate the more substantial sandwiches that Carol had brought and over tea, Anne's mood and complexion perked up. They had another nice conversation, and the visit was coming to an end. Anne handed Carol the check made out for five hundred and eighty-five dollars.

The trip home was uneventful as always, but Carol couldn't work. Her mind was on so many things that none could be put in any order. There was too much going on in her life then. The work was never ending, and Carol worked harder the harder it got. Her daughter was doing well at university, but graduation time was getting near. And her husband was back home in Blind River. Carol thought that she just couldn't do this trip again. She had become very fond of Anne and the visits were a tonic for her, but Carol would have to move on.

In Toronto, the pace of the campaign for the foundation was picking up and Carol was so busy that a month went by before she knew it. She thought of Anne out there in Glencoe and quickly pushed her out of her mind.

She still had that feeling that there was more to the story of Anne Semple, but she had no more time to think about it.

That's when the call came in from Anne.

"Hello, how have you been, it's been a while" Carol started the call.

"Hello Carol, I have been ill, but I feel better now" "I need to see you right away, can you come for a visit?" "I have a very big check for you this time" "can you come tomorrow?"

It was Friday and there was a function going on that Carol had to attend on Saturday.

"I can't come tomorrow Anne". "There is a meeting that I just have to be at".

"Oh, that's too bad" Anne's voice trailed away and there was silence.

Carol thought about telling Anne that she just couldn't make the trip any longer. That perhaps they could send a courier for the check.

"I really need to see you soon" Anne pleaded.

Intuition took over. "How about if I come out on Sunday" Carol asked.

"I guess that will do" said Anne and they said their goodbyes.

Carol took the train Sunday morning early intending to visit with Anne as always but tell her that they would have to make other arrangements in the future. They could always talk by phone, but she would no longer be able to make the long trip out to Glencoe. When Carol arrived at Anne's house the rain was falling hard, and it was cold. The house looked like it had been abandoned for years. Climbing the stairs and ringing the bell Carol shook water off her hat and coat. Anne arrived at the door after minutes and Carol was taken aback by the change. Anne had grown smaller, her face more pinched and grayer. They walked through the house to the kitchen and Anne turned on the kettle. Carol sat at the table and took note of an envelope with her name on it. That's different she thought.

Anne slowly poured the tea and they talked about recent events in their lives. Carol just couldn't bring herself to say the words that would disappoint this sweet old woman. Not in the condition she saw. Anne related that she had been quite ill since the last visit.

"Why don't you open your envelope now?" Anne finally came to the point.

"Sure, I will" Carol said. She reached out and turned it over. Opening the flap, it was not sealed, she took out the check. It took a full minute for her to focus on what she was actually seeing.

"This is exceptional!" She said as she looked up into Anne's eyes.

"Yes, it is dear" Anne said.

Written on the check in Anne's quivering handwriting was the sum: $1,000,004.00 dollars. Carol had to read it over and over again. In cursive it read One million and four dollars. The hardest part to take in was that it was made out to her, Carol Ethier, not the foundation. She thought it was a mistake, then she thought no, I can't take this. It took a while for Carol to get her composure.

"I can't accept this" Carol was eventually able to get out to Anne.

"Of course, you can, it's for you and your daughter" Anne said.

Carol thought about the possibility. This was more money than she had ever seen or heard of. What it could mean to her and her daughter, the changes it would bring to their life. She couldn't do it. It just wouldn't be ethical.

"That is very thoughtful of you Anne, but I just can't take it". Carol smiled and held Anne's hand. "You have to change the payee to the foundation, not to me"

Anne protested. "This is all of the money that I have, and I want you to have it." "It's for you and your daughter." "You must take it".

Carol talked softly and kindly to Anne for the next five minutes. She explained the ethical dilemma that it would cause for her. She finally convinced her by stressing how the money would help so many people. Anne changed the payee.

Carol spent the rest of the afternoon with Anne and made sure that she felt most appreciated for this marvelous gift. Anne assured Carol that the check was good and that she had talked to the man at her bank. It was Carol's intention to leave on the three o'clock but she now had to take the last train at five-thirty.

"I'll call you during the week" Carol said as they hugged goodbye.

"Thank you, Carol," was all Anne said.

The next day at the office Carol decided to deposit the check at the bank without making a big announcement. After putting together the form she left for the bank. The deposit was made, and a receipt taken, Carol walked back to the office. All that was left was to drop the receipt at the comptroller's desk and get back to work.

The news of the gift from Anne went off like a bomb in the office. This was by far the largest gift ever made to the foundation. Entire campaigns brought in forty or fifty-thousand dollars in corporate gifts or multiple payroll deductions. A single gift of a million was just unreal. Carol was the star fundraiser now, the golden child.

There was nothing easy about the way Carol did things. It all came from hard work. She knew no other way. There was no university for Carol. Everything she learned came from the grit and determination acquired from her upbringing. There was no inheritance for her other than that grit that came from the Tapps and Reeds carving out a living in Kynoch. It came from the fortitude her mother showed when she was widowed with three kids and a farm to run. That quiet strength was her legacy, and it took Carol to high achievements.

A couple of days later Carol took a call from Glencoe. She had left her business card and the man calling had found it on the mantle of Anne's house, propped on a candlestick. He was the funeral director and was putting Anne's things together.

"Did you know Anne Semple?" He asked. "I'm handling her funeral arrangements".

Anne's check cleared on Friday. The viewing was set for the following Monday. Carol planned to take the train out again. It was the last time she would ever visit Glencoe.

At the funeral home Carol met two older ladies sitting near the coffin.

She introduced herself and asked: "Were you friends with Anne?"

"No" they said "we just come to these things"

There was no one else there. Carol stayed for a few minutes. She spoke to the funeral director on the way out. Anne had no family or friends. There was nobody for her but Carol.

UNCLE EARL

The flash from the end of the rifle lit up the pasture for an instant. Then the blast echoed back from the far away hills where they were aiming. When Carol's ears cleared, she could hear Uncle Earl's laugh and she laughed too. It never failed to make her laugh when he did, and they laughed a lot. He was standing over her in the moonlight holding the .30-06 that flew out of her hands as she was knocked back on the seat of her pants. He reached down and pulled Carol's eighty pounds onto her feet like he was lifting a dead partridge.

"Kicks a little bit harder than your .22, eh?" Earl was still laughing and so was Carol.

"Let me try that again" She said, and Earl slid the bolt back ejecting the brass shell. Pushing a new cartridge into the chamber Earl pointed the rifle towards the hills in one hand and Carol stood behind it.

"Now pull the butt back into your shoulder tight" He said.

Kicking Carol's right foot lightly, Earl instructed Carol to step back and brace herself on that foot. He flicked off the safety and left the heavy gun resting in her hands.

"Squeeze the trigger, don't pull it". POW!

Carol lifted the knob and slid the bolt back just like she saw Uncle Earl do it. The smoking brass shell twirled away, and Earl laughed. They both laughed.

After a few more shots were fired the fencepost fifty yards out in the pasture rocked back indicating a hit. The next shot Carol took aim and fired. A chunk flew off the fencepost.

Earl looked down at Carol and said seriously: "If you guys are gonna eat this winter, you're gonna need a moose".

Uncle Earl had taught Carol to handle the .22 rifle soon after his brother, her father, was killed by the tractor explosion. She was able to pick off a partridge out of the pine trees before she turned eleven years old. He taught her to shoot the head off to save what little meat was there. It put some food on their table. When she mastered the 16 gauge shotgun, he had her taking them on the wing . Her father's .30-06 was a big gun meant for killing big game. That's what they intended to do.

Earl Tapp was a veteran of the Canadian army who served in World War II. When Carol had first seen the red lines that crisscrossed his chest, arms, and stomach she asked him: "What happened to you?"

"I can't talk about it" he would only say.

Carol asked her elders, and the answer was shrapnel, whatever that meant.

When Earl came home from the war, he married Aunt Muriel and they settled in Iron Bridge. He made his living as a guide for the men that came from Toronto or Detroit and beyond for hunting and fishing. Earl was an outdoorsman from the time he was born into the area north of Huron. He knew the lakes and streams where trout and pickerel were plentiful. His vast knowledge of nature and wildlife brought men to his camps year after year. They knew that Earl could bring them to trails where the moose, deer and bear wandered. They paid good money for the privilege.

Uncle Earl was there for Carol and her family when they needed a man the most in their lives. After Garnet was killed there were things Earl needed to teach them to survive. Carol was the strongest of the kids and Earl taught her the most. Carol adored him for it. He came to the farm when he was able, and he took Carol away hunting or fishing or just showing her how to navigate in the bush. She needed to get away from the house and was eager for the learning.

When the family went to town they would stop and see Uncle Earl and Aunt Muriel if they were home. Carol had such a great time. Mother would warn Carol not to laugh at Uncle Earl's antics, but she just couldn't help it. The butt of Earl's jokes and teases was usually Muriel. Earl had a Myna bird for a pet, and he taught it to talk. Of course, Earl had a colorful vocabulary and so did the bird. When company would come through the door, the bird would scream.

"GET THE HELL OUT OF HERE. WE"RE NOT HOME!

Earl would laugh and laugh, and the bird would repeat, repeat, repeat.

Aunt Muriel was a beauty but unfortunately, she was very short and very round. One day Aunt Muriel said to Edna and her sisters:

"I don't know if you have heard or not, but I have come into a little money"

Everybody knew of course. News like that traveled in the small town faster than the party line would carry it. Muriel had won a million dollars in the Publishers Clearing House Sweepstakes. I wonder if Ed McMahon traveled the thousands of miles up to Iron Bridge in the middle of nowhere with a big cheque and at Muriel's front door the bird told him to get the hell out.

Muriel loved to play cards for money and Earl would make the games so much fun. Carol would join the games when she was older and always sat across from Earl. Earl gave Carol the eye and Carol smiled looking down at the cards.

"Are you cheating Muriel?" Earl asked.

"MURIELS CHEATING-MURIELS CHEATING!" the bird squawked sitting over Muriel's shoulder.

Muriel looks up at the bird protesting "I'M NOT CHEATING!" and the laughter rolled.

Earl's brother, Carol's Uncle Ed lived across the road from the farm in the home of her paternal grandparents. They passed away soon after Garnet was killed. Ed remained there but the family saw more of Uncle Earl. Uncle Ed had suffered from polio as a youngster and was severely physically challenged from it. Uncle Ed could be bitter and cranky, although respected, he was not beloved by Carol as Uncle Earl was. One year Uncle Ed called for a big family reunion to be held at his camp, a remote and drab little place. Carol didn't want to go and neither did Uncle Earl.

On the day of the party Earl announced: "We have a hunting trip planned and Carol and I have to get some meat for the winter"

Carol and Earl skipped out into the woods and had a great, happy day.

Earl bought a beautiful camp from an army buddy on Blue Lake. It was called Blue Fox Camp and located many miles north of Blind River. It was accessed best by float plane, but you could get there by driving to and hiking down the old logging roads. There was a main lodge, six cabins and a cookhouse. Carol loved it there but there was no money for a plane ride, so they had to hike. The guests came from all over Canada and the US to fish the lakes for trophy sized brook, lake, and rainbow trout.

It was now October, and the days were getting colder in the morning and warming after noon with the sun setting earlier. Leaves were mostly down from the alders and the first snows were beginning to fall. Uncle Earl came through the door of the farmhouse on Saturday morning and Edna poured the coffee.

"The moose are starting to move around up near camp." Earl announced. "Carol pack your wool clothes and get the rifle and ammunition together. I want to be on my watch when the sun comes up tomorrow".

Carol looked at mother and waited. When Edna nodded, she was thrilled. No work and no church tomorrow!

"You'll need to milk the cows this morning and clean the stalls when you come back" Edna ordered.

Carol was awakened the next morning by the sound of Uncle Earl stoking the fire in the stove back to life. The cabin was freezing, Carol got up and moved to the fire.

"What time is it?" She asked. Shivering, she rubbed her arms and hands to get the blood moving.

"It's three and we need to get moving" He croaked. Bacon was already sizzling in the pan.

"Get dressed and mix the batter" Earl said but Carol was already moving.

When she was dressed Carol cracked two eggs into the flour, poured in milk, oil, salt and powder. She stirred it up and poured the first cake onto the bacon grease. Flipping it just seconds later it was cooking fast. Earl's cake was done and now hers, they ate a big breakfast of crunchy bacon and hot pancakes, lots of butter. Carol washed it down with milk and Earl coffee. When they were done Earl put two thick slices of white bread on the grease to soak it in. Carol turned the key to open a can of Klik and shook out the meat. Earl sliced four slabs of the Klik and taking the bread off the grease he made two sandwiches, wrapped them in wax paper and shoved them into a canvas bag.

Earl said nothing as he slung the bag over one shoulder and his rifle over the other and moved to the door. Carol imitated his every move and followed, silent as the door opened into pitch darkness and bitter cold. The hike to Earl's watch was three miles up and then down towards a lake. He had the perfect spot and it never failed to attract game. There were two trails below that converged and then split towards the lake. The wind was always off the lake and uphill so that they couldn't be scented. They reached the watch as the sun was just coloring the eastern sky with gray, night hung on above them. Earl's voice was a low whisper.

"Load your rifle, four shells, we have an hour until they come". Earl said and Carol obeyed.

"Take one knee and be ready to stand and fire" Earl said after ten minutes.

Carol knelt and heard the frost crunch under her. She said nothing.

"When I touch your gun, I want you to stand, aim and fire" Earl said under his breath.

It seemed to Carol that they had waited two hours now. Her legs were aching. She felt like she couldn't hold still for another second.

The sun was up now, and the light was good. The lake was still shrouded in fog, but the trails were clear. She heard it before she saw it.

The bull was moving as if he were trying to make a ruckus. They watched him charge a tree and rake it with his antlers. He'd back up and charge another one, rake it. At fifty yards out the bull stood for ten minutes and stared right at them. His nostrils were flaring in and out and they froze like statues. He must not have seen or smelled them, so he trotted down the trail and stopped to look at the lake where his cows were probably waiting.

It was broadside to them now, sixty yards out. It was as big as her Clydesdale Dan, the antlers looked like airplane wings. When its head turned towards the lake, Earl touched Carol's gun. She stood and aimed at the dimple behind its shoulder, about the size of a partridge's head. Just like Uncle Earl said it would be, she fired.

Earl stood and stared at the fallen mass of brown fur on his watch for a good five minutes. It didn't move. He walked towards it without a word. Carol ejected the spent cartridge and left the bolt open. Propping the .30-06 against a tree by Uncle Earls gun she followed him down. She stood by the fallen giant with her eyes wide. The foreleg was taller than she was. Earl just made sure the beast was dead.

"Your gonna need to gut it now" Earl said finally

"How are we supposed to do that". "This thing is huge!" It was the first words Carol spoke since breakfast.

Years later when Earl Tapp was dying Carol would sit with him in the hospital. They talked about family, old times, the fish they caught and the moose.

"What a shot" he said: "What a great shot".

"What can I get for you Uncle Earl?" Carol asked this question on every visit.

One time towards the end, Carol asked again. Earl held up his hand with finger and thumb spread three inches apart.

"About this much whisky and a cigarette" Earl laughed and they both laughed.

On the way home Carol stopped and bought a pack of cigarettes, first and last time she ever did that. At home she took a clean canning jar and poured three inches of rye.

"Don't tell Aunt Muriel that I did this" Carol warned as she hid the booty beside Earl's bed.

On her next visit Earl told her that he got about half the whisky down before they caught him. Later he was smoking a cigarette when the nurse came in.

"Do I smell smoke?" The nurse said.

"I don't smell anything," Said Earl

Seconds later the bedsheets went up in flames and Earl and the nurse are beating it out. Carol and Earl laughed their last laugh together.

Uncle Earl never went to church, his cathedral was the outdoors. At his funeral, the speakers included a Catholic priest, a Methodist minister, the head of the Ojibway tribe at Algoma and the leader of the United Church. They all spoke long and lovingly of what a kind and righteous man Earl Tapp was.

IRVIN

The new decade turned over to the sixties and Carol turned thirteen years old. It was both a happy time and a sad at time. Carol was helping with the preparations for her Uncle Irvin's wedding. She was going to be a bridesmaid in the wedding, so she would get a new pretty dress. But she was losing her best friend, Irvin. He was what they called a Sunday afternoon child, born later in life to Grandma Reed. He came to stay at the farm with his mother when the wedding was imminent. Irvin was a logger and spent most of his time up north in the camps. When he did come back, he would stay with them and he was fun.

The winter before the wedding Irvin was staying at the farm. The neighbor at the next farm, Roy Berry, asked Irvin to drive a truckload of logs down to Sault Ste Marie to a mill. Irvin could use the money, so he said sure.

"Would you like to come along for the ride Carol?" Irvin asked. "We could have dinner at the truck stop too"

Carol was thrilled, she had never eaten at a restaurant in her life. So happy that Irvin had considered her for the ride, she could not wait for the next day to come.

The lumber was already loaded when Carol and Irvin walked to Berry's place. Snow and ice crunching under their feet as they strode into the yard. Irvin climbed up into the cab and turned over the hulk of a truck. It was an old beat up flatbed, but it fired right up. Carol grabbed the handle and pulled herself onto the step. Pushing the button, the door popped but had to be pried open with creaks and thunks. Irvin had to come around and push it closed. They were off and Carol was excited, looking forward to the adventure.

The two hour ride went by too quickly. At Sault Ste Marie they drove straight to the mill. Waiting their turn to be unloaded, Carol was thinking about dinner, what could it be. It was late afternoon before Irvin came out of the office with Berry's cheque. The weather was clear, but the temperature was dropping. Night fell as Carol and Irvin turned into the diner, there were trucks parked all around it.

After they slid into an open booth Irvin picked up a menu and asked. "What will you have?"

In a little voice, barely heard above the din Carol asked. "Can I have French Fries?"

Irvin flashed a big smile and said: "Sure, would you like a burger with the fries?"

It was too much to even imagine. Carol's mother cooked burgers for the men that stopped in at the gas station where she worked. There was never one for Carol though, she could only look at them and salivate.

"Yes, I would like a burger" came the little voice back.

"And what would you like to drink?" Uncle Irvin asked his little friend.

"Can I have an orange pop?" Carol had never had one, but she wanted it. Irvin ordered for them both. The pop came with a white paper straw in it.

They talked about little things and Carol was just so amazed that Uncle Irvin was treating her like a grown up. It was the time of her life up until then and she loved him for it.

When it was time to leave, they went out the door to a frigid temperature near forty below. The truck growled to a start and the gears ground into low. The sides of the road were black on the way back home, but the sky was filled with stars. It was just past Thessalon when the truck stalled for the first time. Irvin got out and scoped out the problem, frozen gas line. He got it thawed and gas flowing, they were on the way again. Two miles further on the truck stalled again. Irvin got it going but now he was regretting that he took the Station Road to Kynoch. There was no help out here on this road. The truck stalled three more times in the space of five miles. The last time it did Uncle Irvin climbed back in the cab and told Carol: "We're going to have to walk the rest of the way".

It was over two miles to the farm from there and freezing with a bitter wind. They walked like it was a death march. The exposed skin on their faces behind a scarf was pained and then deadened. Their feet and hands were like blocks of marble. Somehow, they made it to the farmhouse door, Irvin pounded on it with dead hands.

Irvin's mother woke up and threw open the door. "My god you're dying!" She cried.

The women put Irvin and Carol's blue feet in cold water next to the wood stove. It took some time to thaw them out by feeding them hot tea and soup. It almost killed her, but Carol was so happy that Uncle Irvin took her on that trip.

Most of the livestock was gone now and Carol spent more time concentrating on school. A good student, she was looking forward to entering high school in the fall. The Granary was where they kept the feed, and it was running with big rats. Carol was emptying the traps of dead rats and resetting them when Irvin came by on his way out to town.

"I couldn't do that" He said, "I'm afraid of them".

Carol picked up a rat still alive in the trap with a stick and chased Irvin away screaming. It was funny she thought at the time but later when he was gone, she felt bad. He was her favorite Uncle.

When Irvin came back to the farm next day, he whipped Carol with a rubber hose for that. Her heart was broken. There was pain from the whipping, but the heartache was worse. That he would do that to her was hard to understand. But that was the way they must have been raised. Uncle Irvin married and moved far away. Carol felt like she lost her best friend.

Years later Carol had moved to Toronto and Uncle Irvin was close by in Kitchener. When Irvin was dying Carol would drive out and bring him dinners. Once she sat down and wrote out all of the memories that she had with him. The writing just flowed from her pen, but it took her two hours. He was sleeping when she got there so she left the dinner and the writing on the kitchen table.

The next time she saw him he said: "Must have taken you weeks to come up with all those stories"

"No" She said. "Not at all"

High school was not very memorable for Carol. She describes herself as painfully shy. The trip to Blind River involved a ride in Tulloch's Taxi. It was all girls and only one boy, most of the boys went to work at their farms after grade eight. Lloyd Allen drove the taxi for them the fifteen miles to and from Iron Bridge despite being physically challenged from polio. He was painfully thin and misshapen, and Carol wanted to give him food.

"We don't have enough food for ourselves," Said Mother. "Lloyd makes good money in his taxi; he can buy his own food".

From Iron Bridge the kids would board the bus for a sixteen mile trip to Blind River District High School. There were three classes in each grade at the school, A, B and C. The classes were ranked just like that with the best students in the A's. That's where Carol met her friend for life, Veda. They were in the A class together from then on. Veda had great clothes and Carol envied them and admired her. They came from very different places and situations but at that time and place they bonded. To this day Veda and Carol are still close despite living thousands of miles apart. They talk on the phone frequently and visit each other when close.

At age sixteen Carol begged and bothered her mother to let her spend a Friday night sleep over at Veda's. Edna finally relented and the girls planned for the next weekend.

That night Veda was busy getting her hair done up and make-up on just right.

"What are you doing all that for when we're just going to bed?" Carol asked

"Oh, I'm just practicing." Veda would say: "Want to try some?"

Carol had never worn make-up before, and she didn't now. It wouldn't be until after she was married that she did.

A little while later two boys came to the door, both very handsome. Veda asked them in like she was surprised to see them. She had been seeing the Smith boy for some time and the boy with him was his buddy. They talked for a few minutes, Smith's buddy didn't say much, and the boys left in a hurry.

After they left Veda asked: "Well, what did you think?"

"What did I think about what?" Carol answered. She had no idea what Veda was talking about. Up until now all Carol was interested in was keeping Mother happy and hoping that the garden didn't freeze.

"The boy that was here, Andre." Veda said laughing. "I was trying to set you two up."

"He's very good looking." Carol said after a minute. "But he couldn't be interested in me, he's five years older than us." That boy would be Carol's husband two years later.

He called the house soon after their first meeting. Edna would answer the phone and then hand it over to Carol along with a stern look. They started dating and he would drive out to the farm in his own car. It was thirty-five miles of bad road each way, but it didn't discourage him. He was working in the mines and making good money.

Andre invited Carol to the senior prom coming up at the school. She got a gown to wear from her cousin Jean and the two girls dressed and got ready at Veda's house. They had a great time that night. The music was Rock-n-Roll and some slow dances mixed in. Towards the end of the night there was an election called out for the king and queen of the prom. The student body

66

did the voting. The names were announced, and Carol was absolutely stunned when her name was called as the queen. She had no idea that she was not only beautiful but well-liked by the entire student body too.

The school year was coming to an end and plans were being made for the future. Veda was going to be attending a college in Michigan. For Carol there would be no university, there was no money for that. She took a job as a teller at a bank in Sault Ste Marie. The idea was that she and her sister would save money and buy mother a second-hand car. They were able to do that, a good used car. Carol was almost a hundred miles away from Iron Bridge and rooming at Aunt Blanche and Uncle Herb's house. Andre and she continued to see each other when they could.

Veda and Carol stayed in touch all through the time that Veda was away. When she came home for breaks, they would always see each other. Over the sixty years since they first met there have been the inevitable changes. Moves away from Blind River were made. Relationships came and went. In spite of distance or constraints in time they always stayed close. Like every single person Carol ever came to call friend and there are hundreds, Veda and Carol have stayed friends for life.

Aunt Blanche

Sault Ste Marie (Soo Saint Marie) is a busy little port city that sits on the St. Mary's River at the US-Canada border. The Soo Locks carry lake boats past the rapids from Superior to Lake Huron. The boats then move south into Lakes Erie and Ontario carrying the products of the mid-west and prairie provinces to the world. This is where Uncle Herb and Aunt Blanche lived after traveling all over the world for his work. Herb was a self-taught construction engineer having never finished high school. He built bridges, dams, canals, and the locks.

Carol went to live with them after finishing high school. She loved Aunt Blanche like a second mother, Blanche loved her back even more. Herb and Blanche were more sophisticated than all of the other relatives that Carol had. They understood Carol's desire to learn and grow beyond the circumstances of her childhood. They supported her in every way where some of the others discouraged her. Carol grew very close to their daughters, Jean, and Nancy. She later was a roommate of Nancy and her husband at their home. She is still close with Jean, emailing with her weekly.

The job she got in The Soo wasn't her first work experience. Besides the farm work that started at age six, she and Colleen and cousin Vera also worked summers at a tourist camp. That was hard work at low pay, but it helped mother keep up the house after the animals were all gone. The camp, called The Outpost, was owned and operated by a family from Ohio. They were rigid taskmasters to work for. The girls were picked up after the last day of school. They got a small room to share above the laundry building. The lodge had eight guest rooms and a dining room. There were also eight cabins and Carol and her cousin had to clean them all. Breakfast was at five and then it was work all day until eight o'clock. For this they were paid $25.27 every two weeks. On the day before high school was to start in the fall they were driven back home by this family and dropped off without so much as a goodbye or thanks.

One morning at The Outpost before five Carol was walking past the garbage cans half asleep. There was a low rumble near the cans, and a growl. Turning around she saw a big black bear standing three feet away. Scared out of her wits she raised her arms waving and yelling at the bear. She knew running would have surely killed her. The bear gave her a look like "Thanks for wrecking my meal" and lumbered away. Still shaken she went on to breakfast. Uncle Earl had taught her well.

The family had a Siamese cat that was just as miserable as they were. Carol would be cleaning in the lodge and the cat is up on a shelf staring at her. When Carol got near to that cats perch it pounced on her head scratching. One time the cat leaped at her and dug in with claws. Carol grabbed a handful of it by the fur. Pulling it off she threw it into the deep freezer. After walking away and thinking about it for a few minutes she realized that she could get in big trouble. Going back and opening the freezer the frosty cat jumped out shivering on the floor. That cat never bothered Carol again.

As I said, Carol started working in Sault Ste Marie at a bank. She got the job by walking in and talking to the manager. He was a big, gruff man and he asked her: "What would be your qualifications for a job here, girl?"

"I'll do anything that's needed, and I'll work harder than anyone." Said this painfully shy farm girl.

"How are your math skills?" He asked.

"Excellent" She replied, and they were, her best class in school.

Then Carol came up with the line that would serve her well in many job interviews later: "You will never regret hiring me." She promised him.

After a day with cursory training, they made her a teller behind the wicket to handle the transactions people would bring in. She liked the work and especially liked being able to meet and talk with the customers. It pained her to have to speak louder but she forced herself. She was enjoying overcoming the shyness that was her previous personality.

One morning, three weeks into the job, just after opening, a big man walked in with a ski mask over his head and a long rifle in his hand. He went right to Carol's wicket and pointed the rifle. Carol handed him a stack of ones and he tossed them back at her.

"Give me the twenties" he growled at her. She handed over the money and pushed the silent alarm button on the floor. The man got out of the bank and disappeared. Of course, Carol was scared silly but under control. The teller next to her, Joan, was crying and wailing.

The manager standing there said to Carol: "You're the one with the gun in your face, why aren't you losing it?"

"I told you that you wouldn't regret hiring me." She replied.

She was told that the man was arrested at his place of work later that day. She gave her notice and left the bank a week later.

She had then lined up a job with Weyerhaeuser, the big lumber corporation. She was just one of the office girls and it was extremely boring. The job was just shuffling papers all day with no interaction between people. She would beg for more work to do and more responsibility, but it was the corporate structure that held her back. Maybe to keep her quiet and give her something to do they decided to make Carol Miss Weyerhaeuser for the upcoming Canada Day parade. She would have a gown made and tiara and ride the Weyerhaeuser float. She also had to participate in the beauty contest. Still somewhat shy and introverted, she felt that she had no place being in this group of pretty girls. It's no surprise that Carol was elected the winner and reigned for a time as Miss Sault Ste Marie.

Edna sold the farm after Colleen and Carol moved away. She got around six thousand dollars for all the land, house, and barn. It was enough for her to buy a house in Iron Bridge, and she moved there with Blaine who was just entering high school. She loved that house and was very proud of it.

Carol and Andre continued to see each other when they could. The Soo was a two hour drive from Blind River where Andre lived. The work in the mine was hard but in spite of the fatigue he made the drive often.

Carol turned eighteen years old, and she got married soon after. What a fight it was put up by Mother and all of the relatives, except Aunt Blanche. The horror was that she was not only marrying a Catholic but a French Catholic too. Edna even brought in the pastor of the United Church to try and talk Carol out of it. The fight went on for weeks but to no avail. Carol and Andre were determined, and they set the date. Aunt Blanche was encouraging and so was Uncle Herb. Again, they knew that Carol was bound for better things.

The wedding came off well in the Catholic Church. After all was done and they got to know Andre better, everyone liked him. The relatives came to love him because he was a really nice guy.

After a honeymoon in the Poconos the newlyweds moved into a rented house in Blind River. The house was old and worn but the landlord put a fresh coat of paint everywhere. It was something that Carol had never seen before. She was proud of how nice it looked when showing it off to her Mother and Aunt Muriel. Edna's house was only fifteen miles away and they visited often. Andre left the mines and took a job at the high school teaching Industrial Arts. Soon after Carol took a job in the library at the same school. It was a short walk from the house to school and they could go home for lunch together.

Andre was well known and liked in the town. He was an avid outdoorsman and had a lot of friends. There were too many days and nights when Andre would be out with the boys. Carol was too timid at the time to raise any protest. As the sun would be setting on a day and Andre not home a growing uneasiness came over her. She tried reading books brought home from the library. As the darkness took over, she found it more difficult to concentrate on reading. Soon she would find herself sitting in the same place staring into the darkness. It would not be until Andre came home that she was able to go to bed and sleep. Now in hindsight Carol describes the feeling as real fear. She recognizes the episodes as a reaction to the trauma experienced in her childhood in Kynoch.

The young couple spent a year at the rented house then they were able to buy a house on a large lot by the river. The cost of the house was five thousand dollars, and it would need an entire rehabilitation. They gutted the place after fixing a large hole in the floor. Andre was very able at the construction and had plenty of friends to help. They soon had the house put back together in great condition to move in. For the first time in her life, Carol had a water view from her house. It definitely had a calming effect that eased the fear she felt on being alone. It became Carol's habit from then on to seek out that water view in her homes.

The first five years went by and they had a wonderful life. They had snow machines for fun in the winter. They would ride into the night and party with friends in the wilderness. Summers they had a boat and trailer for fishing and exploring. Soon they were able to buy a camp on Matinenda Lake. It seemed to Carol that Andre would spend all the time working on the cottage but there was time for parties. This camp was boat access only and sometimes there could be many boats tied up at their place and a huge crowd. They had a steam sauna powered by a wood stove and the guests could fry in the sauna and then jump in that cold lake. Carol did the cooking to feed the crowds.

Andre came from a big family and didn't want to have children at all. Life was too much fun as it was. Then once,

Andre's brother and sister-in-law came to visit. They had two kids and a baby. Carol was crazy for that baby. Andre's brother said to him: "You should get her pregnant. She needs a baby".

Carol had a very short window then to get pregnant and it happened almost immediately

MIKELLE

Carol was in the third stage of labor for the third straight day, and it was getting towards nightfall. This whole pregnancy had been extremely difficult, Carol had spent the last seven months flat on her back and she was now exhausted. Doctor said the baby was breech and the umbilical is wrapped around its neck. The hours went on and on with the doctor flipping the baby back and forth. The work just kept up and Carol went into delirium, she had no strength left. At some point thereafter Mikelle was delivered alive. Not by Cesarian as would normally be done by any modern hospital of the day. This was a natural birth, the way they did things at Elliot Lake Hospital. The way things were done in the north of Huron.

The next day the doctor checked himself into a psychiatric hospital. Carol is unsure whether or not he ever practiced medicine again.

Soon Carol was able to recover, and it wasn't too long. This was the toughest eighty pound woman in Canada. She was terrified that the baby was brain damaged. They brought Mikelle in and Carol checked out all the parts. Her tiny arms and fingers were moving like normal. The legs kicked down, and her mouth opened with a cry. That little voice brought the greatest joy and Carol's heart soared. "My daughter, she's alive".

Andre didn't know how to deal with a baby, and he didn't want to learn. He never bathed her, never changed a diaper, never fed her, or put her to bed. Carol was like a single mother and she loved it. She quit her job at the school library and stayed home and raised her baby. These were the best four years of her life. Mikelle was loved so hard that the relatives wondered if Carol might be spoiling her. The love and affection that may have been missing for Carol from her mother were brought out tenfold on Mikelle.

They did everything together. Her first steps were taught by Carol. She also taught her daughter the kinds of things that trained Carol for toughness on the farm. Carol later thought that she may have been too strict. Mikelle was obviously bright because she learned all these things easily.

They went on cross country ski outings and had picnics in the snowy woods. Mikelle rode on the snow machine bundled up with Carol driving. In summer they walked everywhere hand in hand. Carol showing Mikelle all of the wonders of the world. At the camp on Lake Matinenda, Carol drove the boat and taught Mikelle to fish. They caught bass or pickerel and brought it to shore. She showed Mikelle how to clean them and fry it for dinner.

The four years went by too fast, and Mikelle was now grown beyond a toddler, She would be in Kindergarten when the next school year started. Carol wondered what she was going to do with her time. "I'm going to be alone".

Carol bought a cheap sewing machine as a Christmas present and taught herself how to sew. On a trip to Sudbury, she bought the most expensive piece of purple suede fabric for a reason. She knew that it would be hard to work and that because it was expensive, she couldn't waste it or make mistakes. She made a mini-skirt and matching vest and wore it for years. The expensive fabric was hard to get and that gave Carol the idea to open a fabric shop there in Blind River. She talked to a good friend Claudette and asked: "What do you think"

"I think it's a great Idea" the friend said and that's how the business was launched.

The business was started in the basement of their home. There was no place within two hundred miles of Blind River to find quality fabric and who knew that the people in that small town would buy it. Carol traveled the 200 miles to the city of Sudbury where her good friend Veda was living. She went to the fabric store where she had bought that purple suede expensive fabric. When she asked the owner:

"Can you give me the names of some of your suppliers?"

"No!" The old lady answered, and she meant it. She wasn't giving away anything.

Carol went and stayed with Veda overnight and went back to the store next day.

"You again said the old lady. What do you want?"

"Can't you just give me one name. Even if it's just the button guy" Carol asked.

"I won't give you anything. Get out of here" the old lady was getting angry.

Carol went back to that store again and again until finally the old lady said: "You just will not give up will you"

"No, I won't" Carol said. "I am going to make this happen".

The old lady gave Carol one name, Dimitri and sent her away. He was a traveling salesman of notions. Carol had to pry the phone number out of her.

From Dimitri Carol got a contact for Brown's Fabric out of Toronto. From there the business just took off. Who knew that the ladies in this remote town would want to buy quality fabric? Carol knew, she started making buying trips of eight hundred miles to Toronto and back in the station wagon. Her good taste and sharp eye guaranteed that what she bought she could sell.

The custom sewing business started from Carol's diligence in the sewing that she taught herself. She and Andre would love to go to the Saturday night dances held in their town. Carol would make her own outfits and of course her good taste and eye for fashion made them stylish. Ladies would come into Carol's store on Monday mornings.

"I want to buy the dress that you wore to the dance on Saturday" They would say.

"You mean that you want me to make one for you?" Carol would ask

"No" They would answer "I want that dress"

A new business was born, and it took off just like the fabric shop. Carol was so busy.

The next spring came, and she realized that the fabric and dress sales could tail off for the summer. The area around Blind River was a draw for cottage people that came to town in the summer. They came from the cities and the states to the South for the cooler weather and the beauty of the lakes and rivers. Carol had the idea that a gift shop would give the cottage ladies a place to come to in a town that didn't offer much entertainment. Another business took off in the basement of the house.

Things in the basement started to get kind of crowded now. The three businesses were thriving, and the space had run out. The need for more space sparked by Carol's ambition to thrive and grow the business.

There was a house right in the heart of town on the main street. It was between the liquor store and the bakery. The two busiest stores in town. Carol knocked on the door and when the lady answered Carol asked:

"Have you ever thought about selling your house?"

The woman laughed and said: "Oh no, we've lived here forever"

Carol introduced herself and said: "Well if you ever do, please give call me, here's my number".

She let two weeks go by and then she knocked on the door again. Where she got the nerve to do this who knows. She was just desperate to make her businesses grow.

"Have you given it any more thought?" She asked and made an offer of forty-thousand dollars. At that time, it was a big amount in Blind River.

"Well, I'll talk to my husband, but I don't think so." Said the woman.

"I'll come back in two weeks and we'll see" Carol told her.

In two weeks, Carol returned, and the couple accepted her offer.

The bank approved a mortgage with ease based on Carol's business performance and she was off and running. It was just the perfect location and also a great layout too. A center hall divided the fabric business on one side and the gift shop on the other. She sold only Canadian made gift items for a while but eventually had to branch out. It was also very close to Mikelle's school and she could come to the store at lunchtime and after school.

Carol had become friends with one of those cottage people that came every summer and stayed at their camp on Elliot Lake. Patty helped Carol move into the store and set up displays for the gifts. She has been there for Carol during some trying times that came in the future. Patty has remained a good friend through all the ensuing years and they see and call each other and often.

The dress making business grew to a point where Carol was hiring and training seamstresses and tailors. She was even contracted by the Province of Ontario as a job trainer for the trades. The dressmaking spun off Carol's fourth business. It was as a consultant to men and women in business for wardrobe, style, and comportment. Her customers came from hundreds of miles away and paid well for the expertise. Again, it was Uncle Earl's influence and the grit inherited from the family that enabled her to succeed from nothing but hard work. It was from her Mothers quiet strength that she acquired her perseverance.

When the new shop opened, Carol said that she would run it for ten years, then sell it. That is exactly what she did. Andre was off for winter break from teaching, and they planned for a vacation trip to Cozumel, Mexico. Before leaving Carol contacted a realtor and listed the building and all four businesses for sale.

They had a great time and as usual Carol forgot all about work. She had left the shops in the hands of Sis, a trusted employee and lifetime friend.

Almost as soon as they got home the phone was ringing. It was late and they were exhausted from the trip. Carol tried to put off her realtor on the call, but he wouldn't be stopped.

"We have offers on all of the businesses and the house!" He said, "You're going to want to hear this".

He was right, the offers were everything that Carol was hoping for and more. The sales for each business went to different individuals and the house went to another. Everything moved quickly from there and before she knew it, Carol was retired. Well, not for long.

Carol was too young and ambitious to be spending her time on idle pursuits. Mikelle was going into high school now and had her own interests. Carol was contacted by the owner for a sales position at the furniture store in town. It was the kind of work she enjoyed, helping her customers with design ideas. The sense of style that she had developed was a draw that brought most of the store's clients to her. Earning solely from commissions she did well and had no idea that there was a friction developing. It all came to an end one day when the owner of this family business called her in to his office. The family wasn't happy that Carol was getting most of the sales. She was let go.

Soon after this episode Carol was approached by the Chief Executive from the regional hospital. They had been advised by a consulting firm of the need to hire a director of development. The goal was to raise a million dollars and qualify for an endowment from the province of Ontario to build a new hospital. The board of directors would like Carol to interview for the position. She agreed and prepared a very professional presentation for her interview. One of the other candidates for the position was the wife of the furniture store owner as it turned out. They were a wealthy, prominent family in the region. The board chose Carol and a new and fulfilling career was to about to begin for her.

PICKERING

Tomorrow would be the day that she had been preparing for weeks to come. Carol had packed the car and prepared herself as best she could. She would be leaving the North, all of the friends and extended family; Her mother who was dependent on her; Andre and the house that they had built together. Her daughter, while she finished the school year in Blind River, would be especially missed. Every aspect of the life she had experienced she was leaving, she knew forever.

The relatives had all harangued her with pleas to stay. "Why would you want to leave home?" It was the common question from all. Carol knew the answer but wouldn't say it. She had dreamt of leaving the dull dead end that was Blind River for a long time.

Consciously or unconsciously the desire to move on, to improve, went all the way back to Kynoch. The little girl that grew up the day that her father was killed had to succeed. Her husband, Andre was not working. He had been told that he couldn't work anymore after suffering a heart attack. It didn't slow him down though, he continued with his boats, Ski- Doos, and friends.

After six months, when Mikelle has finished the school year, they would follow her to Oshawa. Andre had promised to move, that was the plan.

"You're the bread winner now" Andre had told her, and Carol took it seriously.

Leaving Mikelle was heart wrenching though. Carol had devoted herself to raising her for sixteen years, steering Mikelle towards womanhood. By building on her strengths, she always set the right examples. Of course, she had achieved that goal as Mikelle was that bright young woman. And it would only be six months until they joined her in Oshawa.

Mikelle was ecstatic about the prospect of leaving that small town.

Next morning Carol backed the old Pontiac out of the driveway. Mikelle stood there waving for a long time. Slipping the car into drive, eyes on the road, Carol couldn't look back. But her eyes filled with tears anyway. Carol had to fight the compulsion to turn around and end this change. The back of her hand pushed the tears away and Carol set her mind for the journey to a new life.

The granite slabs and deep green spruce trees of the North passed by quickly. Carol was soon entering the outskirts of the great city. Her hands tightened on the wheel as the increasing traffic closed in. Driving in the city would be another new experience to be overcome. For now, her fingers squeezed grooves into the steering wheel.

The company had secured an apartment for her downtown in Toronto for the upcoming week. They had mailed the keys and address assuming that Carol could handle it. Somehow, she found the place on her own. No one there to welcome as the door closed behind her.

The unfamiliar furnished unit was silent. Suddenly she felt completely alone and vulnerable.

Waking as she usually did before dawn, Carol realized that she had fallen fast asleep right after lying down from the trip. Unpacking her toiletries, makeup, and the outfit she had planned to wear for the first day she settled into the washroom to prepare. The fact that this was a new place, seemingly a million miles from Blind River, brought a big smile to her face. That determination to move on took hold and she strode out the door to meet the world.

The day would bring meetings at the consulting firm that had hired her. This firm had been contracted by the hospital in Blind River when they needed expanding. The firm recommended that the hospital hire a development director and Carol was their choice.

They hired Carol after the successful campaign she had steered to build the new hospital in Blind River. Of course, they were impressed and offered a good salary and benefits. One important benefit promised was a paid round trip flight home once a month until her family could join her.

The new campaign would involve a goal of raising thirty-million dollars for the Oshawa General Hospital. The rehabilitation and addition project was ambitious but badly needed for the aged facility that served a fast growing population an hour drive east of Toronto. Carol knew nothing about Oshawa, but with her hard work and perseverance, she dug in and would learn all she could —fast.

There was only one friend she knew in the city. Dorothy was a salesperson for fabric whom Carol had met while operating her businesses in Blind River. She learned that Dorothy was staying at a rundown motel which was the only option in town. Carol invited Dorothy to stay at their home whenever she made her trips to the North. They had become good friends and Carol would stay with Dorothy and her husband, Eric, whenever she went to Toronto. They helped Carol with finding a place to live and get acclimated with the move.

Dorothy would remain her only friend for years to come as Carol immersed herself totally into her work.

After a week of orientation in Toronto, Carol located an apartment in Pickering, half-way to Oshawa, and leased it. The work would now begin, assemble a staff, outfit offices. All of this on a much larger scale that what she had done in Blind River. Next up was a Board of Directors meeting and there were a lot of directors. A decidedly male-dominated board with one exception. The feel that Carol got was definitely an "Old Boys Club". The lone female on the board had faded into the background. The Chairman greeted Carol and introduced her to the directors without naming anyone. She was asked to explain the progress to date and lay out the plan for the launch of the campaign. She was prepared but understandably nervous.

There came some questions at that point from a couple of the directors. The impression that Carol got was one of condescending attitudes. Carol answered with some hesitance. When a third question was asked, the Chairman interrupted: "Let's let this manager get back to her work and we'll move on to other business". With that, Carol was dismissed from her first board meeting, and she was grateful. There would be many more meetings in group and one-on-ones to come.

Carol's offices were set up in the gate house of the Parkwood Estate. What once was the residence of Samuel McLaughlin, the founder of General Motors Canada, it was a short walk to the hospital. The McLaughlin family lived there until 1972. In 1989, it was named a National Historic site and McLaughlin a National Historic Person. It's now a museum and architectural gem. The tie in of the campaign to General Motors was obvious and expected. Oshawa was a GM town, thanks to McLaughlin. It once had the largest auto assembly plant in the world. Thousands of jobs in the city came from or depended on the General Motors presence.

The co-chairmen for the hospital campaign were the CEO of General Motors Canada and the president of the auto workers union. Carol worked closely with both. She did meetings with groups of union members and pitched them for support. She met with divisions from engineering or procurement and all of the white collar associates. The executive offices were also generous to the cause with their donations. This led to introductions to the business community at large in Oshawa, all dependent on GM. What Carol learned in the North about fundraising in a small town, she transferred to the small city of Oshawa. That strategy was to saturate the community with your plea and get as much involvement as you can. The staff was busy with enrolling all GM Employees into a payroll deduction system and tabulating and accounting of all the money coming in. Even the GM retirees were involved as a group or individually.

The city gave generously to the cause. The campaign with the goal that looked at first to be unattainable, was now a money raising machine moving toward success.

Early on in the campaign Carol took advantage of the benefit of a trip back to Blind River. It didn't seem as much like home, the commitment to move had been made. She would not be changing her mind. The only service from Toronto was on Bearskin Airlines. It flew to Sudbury so there was still a long drive back to Blind River. The plane was a small prop type and every nuance in the weather was felt in the cabin. She was so terrified that she didn't even notice being sick. The time at home went by so quickly that it didn't even seem like she was there. Catching up with Mikelle about school, friends, and their plans to get together soon in Pickering was the highlight. The reunion with Andre was not so enjoyable. He still was not working but had time and money now for the new snow machine or boat to play with the boys. Riding back to Sudbury for the return flight on Bearskin, Carol could feel an odd undeniable tension between them.

It was soon after her return that she learned that the consulting firm was not going to live up to all of their obligations, including the paid flight home. There were other troubles that caused some concerns to Carol about her new employers. The usual office type conflicts seemed to be larger and went without resolve. There were some slips and misses with paychecks that troubled the relationship. The office would call on too many occasions for Carol to meet at headquarters in downtown Toronto. The commute there was awful as how congested Toronto traffic can be. The grind of the forced travel into downtown only to result in a short inconsequential meeting was frustrating, if not maddening. The signs that she was seeing showed a company that was not well managed. In addition, there was a certain person in the Oshawa office that was sowing seeds with the staff that criticized Carol's management.

Andre had made a couple of trips to the apartment and brought Mikelle, but they were short visits that were too chaotic to enjoy. Mikelle suggested to her father that he should take Carol out to dinner, a movie or something, but he wouldn't hear of it. "Costs too much money," he said.

Near the end of Mikelle's school year, Carol made a trip back with the intention of planning for the move to Pickering. That's when the news dropped that Andre wasn't coming.

"What do you mean?" Carol was stunned.

"I'm going back to work at the school" he informed her. "But your heart, the doctor said…"

He cut her off. "They can't tell me what to do," he said. "I want to stay here and go back to work in the fall".

The feeling that her marriage to Andre was failing came back. She had suppressed these feelings before, but now it was here, staring her in the face.

Hoping for a change of the subject, Carol ended the conversation with: "Well, we'll just have to make the best of a long distance relationship".

Mikelle chimed in: "I'm still moving Mum; I'll see you in a couple of weeks." Mikelle was to become Carol's biggest supporter in all things.

Their reunion was sweet. Mikelle moved into the apartment in Pickering, and they bonded even closer. It soon became apparent to Carol that the small apartment would not be the place she wanted for their new life together. She started looking for their home. After carefully calculating her income and expenses, she determined that she could afford a bigger home. She would just have to cut out the extravagant toys that her husband wanted.

WHITBY

The campaign office by Oshawa Hospital was becoming a busy place now. The small staff that Carol had assembled were tasked with all manner of accounting for the thousands and then millions of dollars coming in. The handling of the payroll deductions alone from GM with its thousands of employees was an immense undertaking. There was then the community of Oshawa in general, there were events to be planned and budgeted for, promotional items were purchased and meeting venues with catering planned. All of this whirlwind of activity coming under Carol's direction was working like a well-oiled machine.

One of the many outreaches that Carol had done was to General Motors retirees. There were a number of groups that identified themselves by factory groups or skilled trades. Some were office groups like drafters or typist and the like. They say birds of a feather, flock together. Carol spoke to them all with her presentations. One day a request came into the office in an odd way. A phone call came in asking that someone from the foundation visit a retired machinist at his residence. He wished to donate.

The young man handed Carol the phone and stood by while she spoke to the caller.

"I don't think we should go there" he said as Carol hung up. "It's in a bad part of town".

"Of course, we will, and you'll come with me" She replied.

Arrangements were made and the next day, Carol and the young staffer left the office. The drive was not far to a residential area near the sprawling GM assembly plant. It was a neighborhood of pre-war era built houses and small apartment buildings. Small stores that were mostly closed down. It was indeed a poorer area. They found the address, a large house that had been converted to rooms for rent. Carol looked up to the porch, a large woman sat by the door with a scowl. The staffer stayed in the car and locked the doors, afraid to get out

"I'm looking for Mr. Rocha?" She asked.

"Room five, second floor" the woman barked.

Carol smiled as she climbed the steps and the woman smiled back.

Rising up the stairway at the side of the entry hall, room five was across from the stairs. Knocking, the door opened right away. Mr. Rocha spoke in an accent that Carol could not understand. It was a mixture of English and a language that was foreign to her. Carol introduced herself and gave him her card and a brochure from the foundation. The small thin man motioned her to come in with a leathery muscled wave of his arm.

Carol made it known that she couldn't understand by pointing to mouth and ear. Mr. Rocha continued to speak but added gestures to indicate that she should wait here. Rocha turned his back and seemed to disappear into a dark corner of the room. Carol looked around the spartan quarters noticing a well-made bed, table, chair and not much else.

When he re-appeared in front of Carol, Rocha held out a tall stack of multi-colored cash. She could see that it was made up of various denominations from fives to twenties. Carol thanked Mr. Rocha profusely and put the stack in her case. It was obviously a large amount. Later it counted out to exactly one thousand dollars. Rocha indicated that he wanted a receipt, so Carol wrote it out on foundation letterhead. Promising that she would bring a proper receipt after counting the cash, Carol turned and made her exit.

About this same time Carol purchased a townhouse in Whitby, a suburb of Oshawa and closer to the office. She took out a mortgage in her name only and her husband's name was kept out of the ownership. They still owned the home in Blind River, but the hope was still there that Andre would join them in Whitby. Mikelle moved in and enrolled for her final year in high school. Carol's work ethic of early mornings to the office and late evening returns had no bad effect on their home life. She devoted her off hours to Mikelle and their new home life. It was rare that Carol would socialize away from their new life together. Andre's visit to the townhouse became fewer and farther between.

The campaign was now in full swing and moving steadily towards the multi-million dollar goal. Soon after Carol had visited Mr. Rocha at the rooming house, she made plans to get him a receipt for his donation. The office learned that Rocha was a Portuguese immigrant to Canada and had worked at the GM plant since his arrival thirty years prior. Carol found a nurse working at the hospital that could communicate in his language.

She would act as translator for the meeting. Arrangement was made for a day and time Carol and the nurse would return to the rooming house.

Climbing the creaking staircase to the second floor they knocked and heard the deadbolt open immediately. Mr. Rocha had a beaming smile as the nurse translated Carol's warm message of thanks for the most generous gift to the hospitals cause. As Carol offered the receipt to Rocha, she planned to leave and possibly never see the man again. Rocha spoke and the nurse indicated that he asked that they please wait just a moment.

Again, Rocha turned away and seem to fade from view. Or maybe they were distracted and looked away to the surrounding room. Carol noticed more details. A well-worn bible was on the table and a shrine to Our Lady. An old clock radio, the lit dial read 2:15 PM. Mr. Rocha materialized again holding out another stack of cash, similar to the first one that he had given. He seemed to be very pleased and happy when they expressed their thanks again for the generous donation. Carol opened her case, stuffed in the cash, and pulled out paper and pen to write a promise for another receipt.

Carol was frustrated at first that she would have to return to the rooming house, given her very busy schedule. Then she remembered her mission and quickly forgot any irritation. Returning to the office, she counted out the cash, twice. It amounted to twenty dollars short of a thousand, odd number. She wondered if Rocha might think that someone had pilfered from it. She took the cash to an accountant and the amount was confirmed. She had the receipt made for $980.00.

Calls for Carol to attend meetings at the consulting firm offices were becoming more frequent now. The hour drive or more to downtown Toronto seemed to get harder with each trip. Especially hard were the lame excuse for a meeting that they were forced to sit through. She couldn't help but notice that there were factions that set up in the offices and infighting was going on. The tensions were palpable, and the mood felt angry. What were small issues got blown out of proportion and were argued in front of staff? There were also some troubles with paychecks being refused by the bank. Some of the staff were complaining.

One morning Carol was in her office at the hospital when a manager from the firm came in and closed the door.

"We're going to submit our resignations to the firm today" he started by telling her.

Carol was taken aback. "I can't quit, I have a mortgage and a daughter to support" she raised her voice in alarm. "I can't afford to be out of work".

"Don't worry" he tried to calm her. "The hospital is taking control of the foundation and firing the firm. We will be working directly for the hospital. You won't be out of work at all".

And so it went that Carol's new life took another turn. They talked out all of the details of what was going to be the transition and then wrote out the resignation letters. Carol was concerned that the firm might make some kind of retaliation but that never happened. Everything went very smoothly so the Hospital and their directors must have had their reasons and justifications in order and legal. The attitude and atmosphere in the office immediately lightened. The mission and work continued on pace. And Hooray! No more trips to Toronto for meetings.

Working with the co-chairmen of the campaign was a pleasure. The head of GM Canada was obviously a man of integrity and a fantastic manager. The Union president was a man that could motivate his membership to contribute as a group to the cause. Working with the Board of Directors to the hospital was a completely different story.

The Board was made up mostly of business leaders from Oshawa and surrounding towns. All older men, company owners, they were used to giving orders and having things their own way. Carol was made to feel that she was the subordinate and that she was to take their advice and direction without question. They definitely were condescending and even belittling at times. Carol knew that to defy the board was to risk dismissal, so she followed directions but still stayed true to her plans.

The Hospitals CEO maintained a suite of offices at the hospital and Carol was called to meet with him on many occasions. Usually, it involved updates on the drive for the goal and what plans might be coming for events and such. Soon these meetings became increasingly more uncomfortable. At first it was an off color remark that was made by the CEO to see a reaction. Subsequent meetings ended with a suggestive remark and Carol trying to keep the situation professional. The man invited Carol for dinner together, business to discuss of course. Carol made excuses to get out of it. Finally at one meeting the executive ended the session by insisting that if Carol wanted to keep her job, she was going to have to sleep with him.

"I'm married and so are you, I've met your wife" She told him indignantly.

It didn't matter, he replied, those were the terms.

She left his office without saying a word. The anger she felt for his blunt remarks soon giving way to a worry over keeping her job. She knew that the Chief Executive could dismiss her without any recrimination from anyone at the hospital. He held that powerful of a position. Having thought long and hard about what she could do, Carol put in a call to the co-chair of the campaign. She considered him to be her boss even though he didn't work for the hospital. She had great respect for him, his assistant at GM put her call through. She asked for an urgent meeting, he told her that he would be at her office early the next morning.

Carol got there early and so did he. They were alone in the office when she informed him.

"I'm going to have to resign from the campaign, it's personal" she said.

Sensing that there was something very upsetting that caused this pain Carol was showing, he pried with a question. "What is it, Carol? We can't lose the driving force for this mission".

She took a moment then blurted out what happened the day before in the office of the Hospital's Chief Executive. His anger was building with every word.

"You're not going anywhere" he assured her. "I will take care of this".

He took her hand and then made his exit as the first of the staff started showing up. It was hard for Carol to focus on the work after that but as the day wore on and the routine took over, things returned to normal. She never heard any more about the incident. The Chief Executive still called her for meetings at his office, but the discussions stuck to business. The edge was hardened though, and this man did step up the animosity towards her. It did make things more difficult for her so Carol just worked harder to bring the goal in quicker.

Carol returned to Mr. Rocha's room with the receipt. He took no notice of the amount, but a funny thing happened. After their short chat Mr. Rocha again seem to melt into the dark corner of the room and for some reason Carol's attention was distracted. Upon reappearing Rocha held out another stack of cash and the strange scenario took place again. This same situation would repeat itself an additional five times. Carol would return to the room with a receipt and Mr. Rocha would produce another stack of cash. He was obviously gaining greater happiness with each donation. The amounts would vary and were always random. Carol never saw where the cash came from and perhaps, she didn't want to. Some power was at work that kept the transactions mysterious and secret.

It was just about a year had passed since Carol took on the mission of the campaign for the Oshawa Hospital. The goal was quickly coming in view for success, ahead of schedule and beyond expectations. It was about this time that the nurse who spoke Portuguese called Carol and told her that Mr. Rocha would like her to come to his room alone. He would be there and waiting tomorrow. Carol was apprehensive but told the nurse that she would be there at 4:00 pm.

The board meeting broke up at 3:00 and Carol hurried to her office, preparing to leave for the day and stopping by Mr. Rocha's on the way home. Parking in front of the rooming house, the street was unusually busy with kids playing, young men just hanging out, women sitting on the porches. Carol climbed the steps and entered the hallway. The scowling landlady was now sweeping the floor, dust hung in the air. They smiled, said hello as Carol lit up the stairs.

Entering Rocha's room Carol immediately noticed two brown paper grocery sacks on the well-made bed. Odd because she had never seen any food or a way to prepare it in the room. Mr. Rocha motioned for her to enter and to look into the bags. Looking down she saw that each was almost filled with different colored denominations of cash. Rocha's smile was huge as he told her in his broken English that it was hers to take for the hospital. She had never in her life seen so much money. There were no words that she could say that were enough. Rocha said it was sure, he wanted to give it. Carol rolled the edges closed on each bag and loaded it under an arm, her case in her hand. She hoped that he would accompany her out, but Rocha sat down in the chair and laughed out loud. Fumbling with the door Carol paused at the top of the stairs, the hallway below was now empty. She paused again at the window in the front door and looked up and down the street. Strange but it now looked deserted, she quickly made it to her car and struggled to unlock her door. She tossed the bags over on to the passenger seat, now starting the car she noticed the children running by. Looking back, she saw the landlady waving from the porch and she mouthed goodbye.

When Carol got home, she took the bags in and spilled the contents onto the dining table. She starts sorting and counting the fives, tens, twenties, fifties, and hundreds into stacks. Divided into piles of a thousand, she was running out of space on the table. It was totaling out to be hundreds of thousands of dollars. When she took the money into the office it was a sensation.

Everyone participated in the counting and accounting for the unusual gift. A receipt was drawn up for Mr. Rocha in an amount over six hundred thousand dollars.

Carol met with the co-chairmen of the fundraising campaign soon after. A luncheon was being planned to celebrate the successful completion of the goal totally many millions of dollars. Carol and the men would be speaking and acknowledging many of the business owners, union stewards and organization heads that got behind the cause. Carol told the two men the story of Mr. Rocha's gift and asked that he could be invited and recognized at the luncheon. Of course, they agreed.

On the day of the luncheon Mr. Rocca sat at the head table and enjoyed his lunch with the president of his union and the man that headed General Motors in all of Canada. Carol spoke first and thanked all of the people that worked so hard with her. She introduced the co-chair and he acknowledged all of his stewards and members who made up the bulk of giving to meet goal. The CEO spoke next, and he called out names of community leaders asking each to stand and be recognized with applause. The two men saved Mr. Rocha for last. They asked Mr. Rocca to please stand and be recognized with applause for his most generous gift. Carol wasn't the only one that cried when they saw a very happy Rocha with tears of joy streaming down his face.

TORONTO

There was no talk of the hospital foundation office closing down. The goal had been surpassed so the intensity diminished but fundraising went on. Carol was wary though and concerned for her job. It wasn't that long ago that she put in her resignation to the consulting firm that had hired her out of Blind River. The entire episode didn't sit right with her. The other manager that resigned with her was not trusted and his behavior towards her proved that out. She had fended off repeated attempts at sexual harassment from a senior hospital executive. After he realized that she would reject his advances, he worked against her in the office. Other co-workers told her that he was spreading negative views of Carol's work and performance.

Carol had always taken advantage of any seminar or workshop offered in the course of her career. Being a self-taught executive in the foundation development field, she couldn't get enough learning and mentoring. It was at a seminar that she met Nancy and they became friends. Nancy let Carol know that the Cancer Society of Toronto was looking for a director of development. She placed a call to the contact that Nancy had given her.

When the call was returned the executive from the Society asked Carol if they could meet that day. Carol was at home in Whitby not feeling well after minor surgery.

"I'll come out to your home" She said, and Carol agreed.

They met and talked for a couple of hours that day. Comparing work and life experiences. Their conversation was more about getting to know each other Carol thought. At the end there was no job offered but Carol felt that they got along quite well.

That night she got the call. Carol was offered the position. It would be a lateral move but a chance to work in Toronto, and a way out of the situation she was in.

"The offer sounds fine but the salary is not enough" Carol replied. "I can't afford to take a step back now with my daughter heading to university". The offer was equal but the move to Toronto would involve higher expenses, and she wanted a raise.

"Let me see what I can do" She heard. "I'll call you back soon".

An hour later the phone rang. The previously offered salary was raised and Carol accepted. "I'll be giving my notice tomorrow and looking forward to the move"

When she returned to the hospital office next, she informed the co-manager that she was going to resign.

"I guess you'll be going back north" He said. It sounded like a condescending sneer.

"No" She said with force and pride. "I'll be working downtown in Toronto".

Carol turned and walked away, hoping to never see him again. She finished out her four weeks' notice and prepared for the next new challenge.

The commute from Carol's townhouse in Whitby to Toronto was a daily grind. What could be a forty-five minute drive more often became a two or three hour slow crawl when traffic on the 401 or parkway jammed. On rare days that she wouldn't need a car, she opted to take the GO train. One trip downtown the car just stopped. She was on the busy 401 highway in six lanes of traffic. Carol was terrified as the cars and trucks sped by on either side. Horns blared as she tried the warning lights that wouldn't work. Nothing but clicks when she tried the key over and over. A feeling of panic was taking over when she realized that there was no escape from the car. Carol closed her eyes, flailed her hands in the air and then braced for an impact. The next thing she heard was a pounding on the side window.

"Stay where you are, I'm stopped behind you. The OPP is on the way" The man was shouting.

The good Samaritan stayed with her until the police came with a tow truck. A failed alternator and tow were a big expense but Carol had it done right away. When the shop in Markham finished, Carol headed for the office in spite of the traumatic morning commute.

Carol's daughter Mikelle was now finishing the last days of high school in Whitby. They were both busy with researching for Mikelle's enrollment in university. It was decided that she would be boarding at a school west of Toronto. The idea of selling the townhouse and moving into the city was now forming more clearly. Her husband was there for a visit that weekend. Carol told him about the breakdown and how scared she was. His only reply was about how expensive the repair was.

The plan for him to join them in the city was now the furthest thing from both of their minds. He was just as determined to stay in the North as Carol was to make it in Toronto.

The same kind of success that Carol achieved at the Hospital Foundation was now showing at the Cancer Society. She led the office by example and the staff there saw how hard work and determination were required of them. Soon after she started the job Carol mentioned to a friend that she wanted a place in the city. Did she know a realtor?

"You have to see my place. I'm going to be giving up my apartment soon" Tina told her about the one bedroom apartment she would be leaving. It was in a tower right on the Toronto waterfront at Queens Quay surrounded by parks and separated from traffic. It would be a short walk to the office. The price was a bargain too. "I'll introduce you to my landlord" Tina said.

They later met with the owner, Tina's landlord, an immigrant from the middle east, maybe Egyptian. He had been highly successful in business and invested heavily in Toronto real estate owning many buildings downtown. Carol explained that she would like to take over the lease.

"We'll have to do a new lease." He replied, "I have been wanting to raise the rent."

Carol then explained her situation with her daughter starting university and all of the expenses that would be falling to Carol to cover. She pleaded for the rent to stay at the same level as a favor to single mother. The landlord finally agreed to let it be for the first year's lease. Carol was now a resident of the great city.

She adapted to the city instantly, reveling in the anonymity of life in the big city. The activity around her was just what she had been striving for.

The work with Cancer Society consumed her as did most of the endeavors that she took on. Carol was finding life in Toronto to be more thrilling than she had ever imagined. What a change it was from the life she knew in the North. The shy and introverted girl was now blossoming into the sophisticated business executive making the rounds in Canada's most worldly city, rejecting that reserved, uninformed person that she was. She was making all kinds of new friends from different places. Her now outgoing personality was recognized as a sweet, sensitive, and caring individual that made fast friends for life. New experiences were opening to her such as the art scene in the city, classical and operatic music. Even sailing lessons on the Great Lake that was her daily view from the apartment. Carol drank in all of the fresh exposures as if she had been starving for them. In fact, she was. She knew that the life she had before, the hard upbringing on the farm, the weariness of the North. They were all behind her now and She was never going back.

The same business philosophy that she had employed to so much success at the hospital was now playing to the larger stage that was Metro Toronto. Carol began making inroads into the huge philanthropic community. She was meeting and relating with some of the controlling interests in the cities thriving economy. Of course, the cause that she worked for, cancer, touched all of the levels of society from rich to poor. All races, and creeds, all ages. Carol could adapt her plea for pledges to all of these areas. But there was a tension in the offices of the foundation that she began to sense from shortly after beginning there. It grew more apparent as each week went by. Soon she realized what was causing the rift towards the end of her first year there.

The city of Toronto hosted the offices of two separate divisions of Cancer Society. Carol worked for the Society of Metro Toronto. Across town in a separate building there was the Cancer Society of Ontario, a province wide operation. There was always a collaboration between the two offices but also some animosity. As Carol's successes at Metro began to grow and exceed the performance at the Ontario office, the tension between the two grew also. Carol was an astute observer of her surroundings and had a keen sense for survival. Lessons that were learned back on the farm, hunting for food to survive with Uncle Earl. Working as a child in the summers at the tourist camp and sending the small amount of pay home. These early life experiences provided the common sense and wisdom that translated to survival in the business world. Carol knew before anyone else that the day would come that the Metro office would be closed in favor of the larger Ontario operation. She prepared for it.

In an effort to promote camaraderie with the mostly female staff, Carol started an exercise class that met at lunchtime. Noticing without saying that most were overweight, ate terribly and were lethargic, she wanted some improvement. A Richard Simmons DVD would be played as Carol led the group. Surprisingly, a lot of them participated and she felt that the desired effect was achieved. She ran the program for the entire time that she worked there.

One of the mid-level staff women was being debriefed by Carol one morning in her office. There was the unmistakable smell of alcohol on the woman's breath. Carol took mental note and planned to monitor the situation in subsequent meetings. At their next review Carol broached the subject by remarking: "Do you smell something strange?"

"No, I can't smell anything" the staffer said. She looked nervous.

Thinking that she should be careful before making accusations, Carol dropped the subject. It was obvious though that this staffer was drinking alcohol during work hours. The staff generally left the office by 5:00 pm and Carol usually worked much later. When the office was empty, she went to the woman's desk to search. In a bottom drawer she found a bottle of Canadian whiskey. Taking it to her office she locked it into a cabinet.

As soon as the staffer arrived for work Carol called her into the office.

"Are you having a problem with alcohol?" Carol asked. "Have you been drinking at the office?"

"No!" The woman shot back. "I would never." "I don't even drink." She said indignantly.

"Well, I have been noticing the indicators in your actions." Carol kept her voice low and soft. "and I found the bottle in your desk drawer."

"That can't be" the woman's voice was rising "and you have no right to be going in my things." It was getting confrontational.

Carol took a firm but quieter tone. "Understand that I can have you fired for this" she started. "I want an explanation."

The woman confessed and broke down crying. "I've tried to quit so many times" she cried. "I know it's a problem, I just can't stop."

Carol held back the displeasure and spoke managerially. "Have you tried Alcoholics Anonymous?" "I think you are going to need counseling if you want to stay on here."

"I can't go to AA" the woman sobbed. "My husband won't let me do that."

Carol was getting the idea that the husband may be the problem. "You could go in the mornings before work. You are going to have to commit to it, I'll go to the meetings with you." Carol offered and she meant it.

"I can't go in the morning, the train schedule, and I live far out. My husband is gonna be so mad." The woman looked defeated.

"Then we'll go at 5 o'clock" Carol was firm. "We are going to start tonight so be ready."

Carol went to that AA meeting and many more after with her subordinate. She was supportive but made it clear that the job was dependent on her stopping the drinking. It brought great satisfaction after many sessions when her staffer would smile and announce: "ten days now without a drink."

When the day came and the announcement was made that her office would close, Carol had already planned for the next position that she would take. Before that day, the signals were becoming much more obvious. The director of development from the Ontario office was now asking for meetings with Carol frequently. Carol knew what was going to happen and fended off most of the requests with a need to work at the fundraising. When she couldn't avoid a meeting, it became a war of wits and Carol was much more prepared for the battle. The director from Ontario would ask for an explanation of how this or that different function or program would run and succeed. Carol would always supply some vague and not detailed description of her methods. Usually nothing that the other director could scratch onto her note pad. The frustration would boil up to a point where this other director would storm out in a huff. It wasn't from any desire for revenge that she withheld her methods. The Cancer Society was a great cause that needed a new direction from their fundraising leader.

When the time finally came and the office was closed, Carol moved seamlessly into the next foundation position. A new office, a new cause but the same grit and determination to succeed.

Just before the lease for her apartment was to expire, Carol visited her landlord's office in order to sign a new one. They sat and talked a bit and eventually he got around to the subject of raising the rent.

"I would ask you to please consider keeping my rent the same" Carol asked. "My position at the Society will be eliminated and I'll be starting a new job right after."

"But I have to keep the rent up with the value of the building" he explained. "The other tenants in your building are paying a much higher rate."

Carol began her negotiation with the careful plan she had used over and over in business.

"My daughter is doing very well at the university, but it is so expensive. I'm handling it by myself." Making the plea at a personal level. "I work hard and long hours in order to give her an opportunity that I never had."

The discussion went on and eventually the landlord agreed to hold the rent at the same level.

"Don't ever tell your neighbors what you pay for rent" he warned. "I'll terminate the lease."

"Of course," Carol replied, "I would never disclose my personal business to anyone."

For the next four years afterward, Carol kept this beautiful apartment. The negotiation of a new lease went the same every year. She always came away with a most favorable result.

KIM & ALICIA

When Carol left the Cancer Society as Director of Development, she had been managing a staff of seventeen individuals. She would answer to a Chief Executive Officer (CEO) within a large organization with worldwide connections. In addition, she was overseen by a volunteer Board of Directors and met often with the Chairwoman of the Board. A typical work week would involve meetings with the CEO and interaction with Board members. A monthly debriefing with the Chairwoman was typical.

As strange as it seems, the subject of Carol's advanced education, or lack of it never came up. Not one of these executives questioned her credentials and Carol didn't think to offer the information. It just doesn't seem possible that a woman with no university degree could achieve this position as a senior fundraising executive. Carol wasn't fooling anyone, there was no con involved in her achievement. There could be no questioning her position because in every way, every day she showed competence and skill at the task.

Carol achieved at this high level beyond any training through hard work and taking leadership. To this self-made woman the need to succeed was born in her from her pioneer family roots. It was imprinted on her from the moment that she watched her father killed. It is a spirit available to all of us immigrants and descendants of pioneers. Start with determination and work hard and we all can achieve our own success.

When the door closed on Carol at the Cancer Society, the next door opened at a new foundation to lead. She took control as Chief Operating Officer of her own division with a staff of two. The situation got off to a bad start almost from the start. Carol began with the usual plan that had always worked for her. Long hours and hard work. After a few days, the two staffers came to her with a suggestion.

"You know, you don't have to work so hard at this" one said.

"Yeah" said the other "you don't even have to come into the office." "We'll cover for you."

These unionized clerical workers went on to explain that the previous executive rarely showed up in the office. He didn't push them to any additional work for increased fundraising and they provided cover for him. They did their jobs but gave just the minimum required.

Carol saw right then that her office was going to need an entire culture change. She also realized that the staff she had would need to change or to move on. She set about to make the change immediately.

"I'm going to be in this office or out in the community every day in order to grow this foundation." She informed them. "I'm asking you both to work with me on this." "Can we agree to it?"

When leading by example failed to motivate these two, Carol switched to more direct methods. When this too didn't change them, Carol began to document the poor performance. The executives of the two divisions that Carol's office funded didn't want to get involved. They weren't interested in making any changes either.

After a sufficient period of time had passed, Carol was now ready to make the changes. She made her first trip downtown to Bay Street. The volunteer Board Chairman was a friendly ally to her. She had interviewed for this position with he and four other board members, and they hired her that day. After she closed the interview with the statement: "You will never regret hiring me." He liked her immediately.

Carol laid out the situation and the documentation that she had amassed. She asked for his blessing and he replied "Of course, and the board will back you up on this."

Since the two union staffers were so closely allied in their work habits, Carol called them into her office together.

"I'm giving you the required two weeks' notice that your positions here at the foundation are terminated." Carol firmly instructed them.

They both seemed shocked and made some complaints. Their voices began to raise, and some curses flew.

Raising a hand and stopping them Carol again spoke in a firm voice. "Let me be understood. You are both no longer working here. That will be all." Carol stood extending an open hand toward the door.

After a little while the two staffers burst back in to Carols office.

"You can't fire us; we have a union." One spoke. "They told us you're wrong to do this."

"I can and will fire you with cause." Carol responded. "I have your personnel files right here."

Carol stood and opened a drawer in her desk. She placed two thick folders on her desk hands down leaning on each.

"I have cause." She explained and looked them both in the eye. "This will be enough."

Later that day the antagonistic CEO of the one organization phoned Carol and asked to meet right away. When Carol arrived at his office, he started in a brisk tone. "You can't do this Carol. I'm going to have to deal with the union" He said.

"The firing is done." She replied, "I can't make any more progress towards the goal with those two working against us." Carol showed him the two personnel files on her lap. "I have all of the negative examples documented here in their files."

The CEO frowned getting redder in the face. "Give me those." He demanded.

Rising from her seat to leave, Carol said. "I will be happy to have copies made and sent to you if you wish." "If there is nothing else?" The question hung in the air as she left.

Carol heard nothing more from him on the subject. She never saw the two staffers again.

Prior to the day that she terminated the two staffers, Carol had placed a call to a Temporary Agency that she had used before. She asked them to send the best executive assistant that they had available. "Would you have her ready to begin work next Monday at 8:30 AM please?"

Carol got to the office early that Monday, as usual and was ready with work assignments for the new assistant. Kim burst through the door in a bustle of activity. Shaking off her coat in a big voice matched by her marvelous personality she boomed:

"Hi, I'm Kim, the agency sent me!" "You must be Carol, I'm so glad to meet you!"

Carol said good morning and shook hands. The whirlwind that was Kim continued.

"Where's my desk?" "Is this it?" She said tossing her purse on it and testing the chair.

"Can I get you a coffee? "How do you take it?" Where's the lunchroom?"

The super confident and competent Kim got right to work. She and Carol hit it off immediately and they started with the procedures and policies that Carol had written up in her mission statement and strategic plan. Carol knew the first day that she had found the right fit to help her succeed. The day would come soon that Carol would hire Kim full time to her staff.

Kim set about organizing the office and procedures in a way that Carol could have only dreamed about. Competence was really not enough of a description. It was as if Kim read her mind and then suggested the most efficient way to bring Carol's plans into action.

This bundle of energy and ambition had another side gig or two always going on. Kim is a talented self-taught musician and performer. Her songwriting genre is an alternative country with a Canadian feel to it. Besides writing songs, she has written plays and a screenplay. She often played at bars and clubs around

Toronto at night and showed no sign of fatigue the next day in the office.

Like a lot of music artists Kim would make trips to Nashville to play at the clubs for free or pass the pail tips. Being discovered and having their creations enjoyed by millions is the dream that they all pursue. Soon after starting Kim came to Carol to ask for a Friday off.

"I have a chance to play at a club in Nashville." She spoke. "I'll work double extra hours to make it up next week." Kim pleaded.

"You don't have to do that" Carol said. "You can have the day off."

"But they'll dock my pay, and I can't afford that." Kim was worried.

"They won't know if I don't tell them." Carol assured her. She knew that Kim would more than make up for it as she did every day.

Kim made a few of those trips in the years that she worked at the foundation. Carol made sure to always let Kim now that she supported her dream.

With the work in the office increasing and fundraising growing exponentially Carol thought that it would be a good time to ask for additional staff. Knowing that she would be met with some disagreement from the two divisions that she funded, she decided to take it up at the next meeting with the board of directors. The board chairman, George, was agreeable to the idea. He held sway with the board, and they agreed that she should add a staff member immediately.

Carol had described to the board that she was looking for a person both very smart and with good computer skills. When the meeting adjourned, one of the members took her aside.

"Carol, I have the perfect candidate for you." He said, "She's a recent graduate with an MBA and she's looking for a job."

"That sounds encouraging." Carol replied. "I'd like to speak with her."

"Alicia is a friend of the family; I've written her phone number here for you."

He handed her the card and they parted ways. "Thank you, I'll call her right away."

On returning to her office, Carol was at her desk when the CEO barged in again unannounced. His habit of forcing in and yelling at her was so unnerving and getting tiresome. This time, perhaps emboldened from her meeting with the board, she acted.

"Aren't you going to answer me?" He was still yelling, and Carol had been silent the whole time.

"I will not be answering you as long as you take that tone." Carol rose from behind her desk and walked to the door of her office. Opening it and standing aside she indicated with a hand for him to leave.

"Are you showing me the door?" He sputtered. "I'll have you fired!" He declared as he rushed out the door in a huff.

Once Carol was calmed down from the episode, she placed the call to Alicia. She answered on the first ring.

"Hello Alicia, this is Carol Ethier, I got your number from a member of the board here at the foundation." "He thought you may be interested in interviewing for a job here."

"Yes, I would." The young woman answered. They planned to meet at the office when Carol had an afternoon free to give it enough time.

It was the early the next morning that a call came in from the Chairman of the Board.

"Carol this is George." He said and he didn't sound happy. "You've been reported."

He laughed at this point, relieving the stress, and told her he got a call from the negative executive at the other division.

"Oh no! Am I in trouble?" She sensed that he was on her side. The tone was lightly sarcastic between the two of them.

"Don't worry about a thing." He said, "I've been thinking that your operation might be better served with an office down here on Bay Street. You'll be closer to the financial center of the city. There's a lot of charitable giving we can tap in to here."

Carol was thrilled to hear the offer and told George so. She asked about where, when and how. George said that it wasn't clear yet, but he would be looking into it and let her know.

Kim had put the call from George through and Carol knew that Kim was upset from the incident yesterday. Carol walked over to Kim's desk after the call was over.

"Well, is that it?" Kim said. "Are we fired?"

"No, that won't happen." Carol assured her. "In fact, we're going to be hiring more staff. I have an interview scheduled for tomorrow afternoon with a good candidate."

Carol does not trust easily but once someone has proven themselves, she has full confidence. Kim and Carol had bonded now as a hard working team. Kim was smiling now.

"And another thing, we may be moving to new offices downtown on Bay Street."

BAY STREET

Carol had been wanting to revitalize the mailer that the foundation used from the first day that she started. It was a tired old appeal for donations that had been printed over and over for years now. The look and feel of it so dated that she was sure that any recipient would assign it to the trash without reading. To Carol's eye for style and design this forlorn looking sheet had no place in her plans. The two union staffers that she inherited were reluctant to change anything and told her they couldn't help. Once they were gone Carol was now excited to put the project into the hands of her newest hire, Alicia.

Kim and Alicia had become friends from the instant they met on staff. Carol could see that they were so much alike and yet such different personalities. They shared an artistic sense and a look of cutting edge style that Carol both admired and displayed herself. Kim was outgoing, vibrant, and extremely efficient. Alicia was more reserved and softer spoken and equally capable. Both were exceedingly intelligent. Carol had decided immediately that Alicia had to be on their team.

It was approaching time now that the foundation was going to be sending the old mailer again. Carol called the printer and put a stop to the order. She informed him that there would be a new design coming to him. It would be a full color sheet on high quality paper and a new text and font. He should forward his pricing to be considered. Alicia got to work on the pamphlet.

That same week a call came in from George, the board chairman. After an exchange of pleasantries George got to the point.

"Carol, Glenn has found some office space in his building here on Bay Street that he thinks you'll like." "Can you meet us down here this afternoon and we'll show it to you." He said,

She was so excited for the chance to move from the toxic atmosphere that was the foundation headquarters. "I'd be delighted George; I'll see you at Glenn's office at one?"

"One o'clock it is Carol, see you soon." They ended the call.

Carol had been to Glenn's building once before for a fundraiser. He was one of many on the board of directors that she liked. His building was an older brown sandstone structure with a beautiful and huge marble foyer. Probably built in the 1920s. Carol was imagining some old style dark offices with windows that didn't open and radiators that overheat. Oh well, she said to herself, it's got to be better than this dull, undistinguished place. And getting away from the battling divisions of the foundation and their CEO's felt crucial.

That afternoon Carol arrived on Bay Street early and waited while George and Glenn returned from lunch. A ride up the elevator to the suite of offices and Carol was surprised, it was nothing like she had imagined. Brightly lit and newly finished, there were large windows opening on two sides. The space was empty of any furniture, but they could tell there would be plenty of room for the operation to expand. Carol's office would be the largest, a corner room with a wide view of the city.

"Well, what do you think?" Glenn asked. "Will this work for you?"

"Oh yes, this is a perfect space." Carol was thrilled with it. "When can we start?"

Glenn explained that he had taken the liberty to order furniture and equipment from a store nearby that sold used. "It's good quality and fairly new." He said, "You'll be able to move your things in here next week."

"That will be fine." She said, "We'll start getting packed and ready to move."

"And one more thing," Glenn added. "it includes a parking space under the Eaton Centre across the street."

Parking in Toronto is tough to find and expensive. The free covered parking was an over the top perk. This new location was almost too good to be true.

Carol, Kim, and Alicia spent the next week packing up the office for the move. When Carol's nemesis there let her know that he was against this, all she could do was smile. In the meantime, she had put in a call to Homa, a woman from Carol's staff at Cancer Society. When the Societies office had closed Carol's, staff had dispersed, and she knew Homa had found work somewhere.

"Homa how are you?" Carol said. "I've been wanting to call you for weeks."

"I'm doing well, how are you, Carol." Homa replied.

They talked for a while and Carol told her about the upcoming move downtown.

"Are you working now?" Carol asked although she knew the answer.

Homa explained what she was doing and the fact that she wasn't happy there.

"Would you like to come to work for me here at the foundation?" Carol asked.

Homa was thrilled with the offer and accepted right away. Carol told her to join them in a couple of weeks at the new offices.

The movers came that Friday, the last of the boxes of files headed out the door. With the offices now empty Carol had one last look. She then made sure to give a pleasant goodbye to the confrontational CEOs of the two divisions. She would need to deal with them in the future. Her fundraising was what funded their work. She was just relieved to be away from the strife and stress of that office.

The next day, Saturday, Carol was at the new offices early. Alone she was unpacking the files and storing everything in place in the new furniture. The board members had done a nice job in selecting some quality things. Carol's office got the best big, beautiful deck and chair set. As a bonus the guys had also included a new updated computer system. She was back again on Sunday to make sure it was just right and ready to start.

Kim came in the office first thing Monday. "Who did all this?" She exclaimed.

"Who do you think?" Carol replied with a big smile. "I wanted to have it all ready for you."

Alicia came in soon after and the team got to work. Kim and Alicia knew instinctively what Carol wanted to have done. Both women are organized and efficient in their work habits. It was their intelligence and artistic abilities that Carol prized for the top quality campaigns that she administered. Carol, the leader, set the pace with strategy and planning.

The mailer was the first thing that Carol wanted to accomplish. Alicia had some ideas ready to review so they worked out the details and a proof was ready. Kim had already gotten the contact information ready for three printers to provide quotations. Once a decision was made there was a new pamphlet ready to mail a month after they moved into the new office.

In the meantime, there were other fundraising events to plan, and the standard business of the foundation attended to. Typically, a response from the mailer would come in two weeks after and petered out after six weeks. The first envelope from this mailer came sooner. Then the pace of responses to the new improved mailer were coming in faster than before. After six weeks the fundraising total dollars from the mailer more than doubled any that had come before it. The updated mailer was such a success that Carol had the idea to modify the next one in six months. It was obvious to her that a new look got attention.

In addition to her skills at design, Alicia was also very skillful at the computer. Carol put her to work with the digitizing of all the operations. When Homa started work there she also improved the flow. The office was now fundraising with greater efficiency, more than justifying the move to new offices.

The parking space under Eaton Centre was a huge benefit for Carol but the Toronto traffic could be brutal. The drive from her apartment at Queens Quay could be a frustrating grind. She could easily walk up Bay Street from home in twenty minutes. She did that in good weather, even in winter. After doing the walk for a while it became obvious that the city had a large population of street people. Carol always looked a panhandler in the eye, and she kept a supply of change ready for those that she felt for.

Shortly after starting at the new office, a homeless man took up position in front of their building. He started with a few meager possessions and over time build up a collection of "his things". He even fashioned a makeshift shelter overhead. Carol would look into his foggy blue eyes and see someone that deserved to be pitied. She started buying him a sandwich and coffee at Tim Hortons just about every morning. There would be no thanks coming from him, just grunts and complaints but Carol could see the appreciation he had. The giving made her feel good too. Once she ventured to ask him what had happen that made him homeless.

"I can't talk about it" was all that he could say.

She asked him once if he went to a shelter to sleep at night

"Can't do that, They steal my things," he said.

The man stayed in front of the building for the entire four years that Carol worked there. If she were away for a holiday, he would growl when she returned "Where have you been?"

It was less than a year now since the move to Bay Street and Kim came to Carol in a state of distress.

"I don't want to leave you, but I can work for a law firm for more money, and I need it." She explained. "It's also four days a week and I need that to practice my music on weekends."

"That sounds like a wonderful opportunity for you." Carol replied, "You have to do what's right for you." Carol was encouraging to her despite the fact that she would miss her.

Carol had hired an executive assistant, Alice, and she was becoming much more proficient now. She'd would also bring on another temporary staffer after Kim left.

It had always been Carol's policy not to socialize with the people that she worked with. When Kim left, Carol stayed in touch as she would with Alicia. She would be an avid fan at many gigs that Kim had at a bar or coffee shop. She helped Kim with her new job, and they remain friends today.

Carol would always be connected to Veda, her friend from their days at High School back in Blind River. They have been close all through the years. Veda and her husband Carl were both teachers in Sudbury, seven hours north of Toronto. Carl is a folk music aficionado, especially Canadian Artists. They would have large gatherings at their house whenever a traveling music act would be passing through Sudbury. Carol arranged with Carl to have Kim perform at a gathering. They drove up together for the weekend.

When the crowd had assembled in the living room it was packed. Kim was nervous, maybe it was the intimacy of the venue.

"I don't know if I can do this Carol." Kim said. "I think it's stage fright."

"Don't worry, these are our friends. And we've come a long way together." Carol calmed her down. "I'll introduce you"

Carol proceeded to present a rousing and funny intro to the star attraction "fresh from Nashville by way of Toronto." It broke the ice and Kim came on and blew that crowd away with her talent.

The office on Bay Street was different now without Kim's huge personality that lit up the day, but the work continued. At a board meeting that included about thirty volunteer members Carol got up her nerve and at the end of her presentation she astounded the room with a request.

"I want each member of this board to give me a name and contact information for one person that had the capacity to give a gift of one thousand dollars or more."

The room went silent except for the sound of drawn in breaths. Carol looked around the room at wide eyes and stunned looks. Then she heard the whispers between them.

Finally, the chairman stood and said to Carol. "That's not something that we've ever heard before."

Carol stood firm; she knew that her request was not too much to ask of these members.

The chairman then addressed the members. "It sounds like something that we should be able to do." "If you don't think that you can comply then you come to me, not Carol."

Returning his attention to Carol he said. "It may take a little time, but this board will get you these contacts and back you up the whole way."

SICK KIDS

It was a couple of days after that momentous board meeting that Carol met with the Chairman. He related that most of the members were shocked with her proposal. The volunteer board for this foundation had an unusually large number of directors. In fact, there were more than thirty, some more active than others. Carol and her staff had done research on all of the directors as potential donors to the foundation. That was the subject of the request for this meeting.

"I'm afraid that I have an unpleasant matter to discuss with you today." Carol stated.

"What is it that's troubling you, Carol?" He showed great concern.

"Through our research it has come to my attention that not one of our board of directors, including yourself, have ever made a personal gift to the foundation!" Carol exclaimed.

He sat back in his chair and thought about what he had just heard for a good minute. Carol sat forward and brought her daily planner into her lap, pen ready to write. The Chairman began first.

"Well, I suppose that's true." He said, "Quite frankly the subject has never come up."

Carol stated this with some authority: "It is my experience that in every fundraising endeavor that I have been employed with, the board members are required to give a substantial gift. I think that it's something that we need to address right away."

Carol's message was starting to make the Board leader uncomfortable. She waited for him to respond. He took some time to think about it.

"I just don't know what to say." He said, "After you just asked each member to give you a name of a potential donor, now you want a gift from them also?" He was sounding incredulous.

"We should expect not only a gift but a substantial one." She stated matter of factly. "These are all men of means that have expressed an interest in what we're doing."

Carol didn't wait for any more objections from Ben. She began to explain her plan.

"My staff and I have researched their giving capacity." "I will be making an in person appointment with each director in the coming weeks and asking them for their pledge." "I don't need to have your help with this, but I would like your support." Carol finished.

"You have my complete support, Carol." He promised. "As to my own pledge to the foundation I will be getting together with my accountant and you will have it in a week." "You're going to get some resistance on this, and I might even get some resignations."

Carol entered the meeting that morning with a sense of dread for what could happen. When she left it was with a feeling of elation. She was starting on a pursuit of one of the most difficult undertakings of her career so far. If she could pull it off with the Chairman, the other directors should prove easier. It was a very satisfying accomplishment.

The office now was at three full time and one part time staff. Kim had left but Carol found a competent executive assistant in Alice. Cheryl and Lisa oversaw the mailings and data input. Grant writing applications were done by all with Carol's ultimate approval. The part time staffer handled the filing, mail handling and the like. It was at this time that Carol brought in the gift that shocked the foundation.

She had been working on a major gift for six months. Making weekend trips by train out of the city to visit with the donor. It was not something that she had related to the board. When the day came that she received the check in excess of a million dollars she was ecstatic. She made an early morning appointment with the Chairman of the Board. His shock and excitement with the gift made Carols many hours of work worth it. He even called a special meeting of the board to relay the good news. Her work bore fruit by prompting the directors to come forward with their own healthy pledges.

There wouldn't be a better time than now to begin the process of meeting with every director on the board. It was not hard at all to make the appointments. The first meetings that Carol made began with a congratulation for her work in acquiring the major gift. Carol was thankful but moved to the subject quickly. In every situation in the first few meetings the board member was receptive. It is never easy to discuss someone's financial circumstances. To come right out and ask for a pledge based on the persons giving capacity was a thing that Carol had to prepare for. She had to fight through a natural reserve and apprehension. It was a performance that was practiced to hide the stress and tension Carol felt each time.

In every meeting at the beginning Carol walked away with a pledge that reached the level she had asked for. Leaving those meeting she felt the same elation as after her first meeting with the Chairman. As the stress drained away there came a feeling of success and accomplishment. It was in the tenth meeting or so that she encountered the first resistance. The director was initially perturbed that he was called out as not contributing to the foundation. When his financial circumstances and capacity to give were brought out he became visibly angry.

"What makes you think that you can look into my business?" He asked indignantly.

Carol could see that this wasn't going well. She immediately began a to explain their methods used in a calm and business-like tone. Trying hard to bring down the level of tension she diffused it with a long and detail outline of her process.

"It's really the practice of every chief executive in the development field." She related. "We use a software designed specifically for this purpose. This is how we identify generous patrons like yourself that care about our cause. We make every effort to remain discreet or anonymous with your information." She finished.

The mood shifted and this director made a pledge that he felt comfortable with. In addition, he provided Carol with the name and contact information of a friend that would be willing to meet with her.

For the next year or so Carol carried out this process of meetings. In every situation each board director made a pledge for a personal contribution. They also fulfilled Carol's request for a contact for the staff to research and ask. The audacious challenge that she put forth at the board meeting became a completed achievement.

It was during her four years at this foundation that Carol worked long hours and every day of the week. Her daughter was away at the university now and came to stay at the apartment only on breaks. There was hardly any time for socializing. When Mikelle was home and went out with friends, she'd implore Carol to join them at a club. Usually, her night ended early on a cab ride home, too tired to party.

Her relationship with her husband also suffered more from their distance and Carol's work. They came to the difficult decision at this point to divorce. He insisted that it would not be contested and done through arbitration. Carol was in agreement; she was not interested in her portion of the house they had built, or any asset tied to Blind River. It was a clean break where both parties went their own way. She still cared for him, but they no longer had anything in common.

Even after a number of years had passed since the divorce was final Carol didn't socialize much. Her time and efforts were absorbed by work and supporting Mikelle. She wasn't at all interested in dating, not that the offers weren't there. The work for the foundation took her in to the company of rich and powerful men and women of Toronto. It was a fact then that there were mostly men at the top of these companies. It wouldn't be a surprise that at some point Carol could find herself in an uncomfortable position. The typical example was a meeting alone in the office of an executive. By keeping the conversation all business Carol could adroitly fend off any advances. There would be many of those.

To say that she was happy working at the foundation would be a stretch. The work was certainly satisfying, and the compensation was most adequate. The achievements that were being made were being recognized throughout the society in Toronto both business and social. Keeping her daughter supported in her studies toward a degree was what inspired her to work so long and hard. Her love of a challenge reinforced the effort.

Her recognition within the community of development directors and charitable foundations was now flourishing. As always Carol would participate in every conference or seminar within the industry. No longer the shy new woman in town that took the back seat quietly. Carol was now being drawn out by her peers as an important leader. At first it was the chance to talk to groups on the work of the foundation. Eventually there was the request for her to do seminars and training on the methods and practices that she employed. The last vestiges of that shy girl that left the farm in Kynoch had disappeared. The leader of this foundation was now a confident and competent executive.

Carol would be speaking to a crowd of twenty-five hundred people at the home of Canada's National Ballet and Opera. The largest crowd by far that she had ever addressed, she was nervous. She was also meticulously prepared taking days to practice. The day before the event she came down with a raging cold. Picking up the phone to call a friend, she pleaded for help.

"I'm losing my voice. What should I do?" "There's going to be hundreds of people tomorrow."

"I'll be right over" Lena said and hung up. Lena was a friend and colleague at the foundation. She brought with her some powerful Asian medicine that her family had used for centuries.

"This will knock it out of you but you're going to sleep. Take it now and go to bed."

When Carol woke up the next morning it was amazing that the cold was gone. The new problem though was that she was covered in hives. A reaction to sulfa in the syrup, Carol found she was allergic to it. She went on to give the presentation in spite of the constant itching of the hives. One of the women in attendance told her after that the talk was outstanding but did she know there were red dots on her face? Not from the hives though, Carol had to laugh at herself. She would use a dot of lipstick and rub it in to add color to her face. In her haste that morning she forgot to blend it in. She did the seminar in clown makeup.

It was at a smaller venue that Carol was presenting a talk about the foundations work. After the presentation was done there were refreshments offered and Carol stayed to meet with some of those in attendance. Standing in a group circled around her and answering so many questions she noticed a man standing aside. He was obviously waiting to speak to her. After a moment she excused herself from the group and approached him. Extending her hand, she introduced herself.

"Hello, I'm Carol Ethier." She said, "Have we met?"

"Hi, I'm John Stevens" He replied. "I know who you are, and I've been wanting to meet you."

Disconcerted somewhat Carol went on to describe her work for the foundation. When John spoke, he went directly to his point.

"Carol, I'm CEO at The Hospital for Sick Children. Our staff has given me reports on your work in the fundraising. I've had recommendations from many of my associates including directors from the board at your foundation. Everyone tells me that you are an outstanding professional."

Carol was thankful but wondering where the conversation was going.

"Sick Kids Hospital is launching a drive to raise nine hundred million dollars and we want you to steer it." He continued.

There it was; the offer was astounding to her. John went on to describe the need for assembling a staff and offices. He outlined a general level of compensation. Carol was barely hearing him as her mind swam with the possibilities. At some point when he paused, she reminded him that she was employed. He offered to speak to the Chairman of the Board for her. He would like her answer now if she could.

Carol thought that she might be out of her mind for saying it, but she asked for some time to think about it. John agreed but asked for a meeting the next day. They met the next evening after she left work. Carol accepted John's offer that evening and told him that she would handle the resignation with her current job. The Board had asked her to come to them before she thought about going anywhere else. She owed them an appropriate notice.

RON

Three days went by before Carol could see the Chairman of the foundation's Board. The only one that she had told about her new position was Veda. Her best friend from Sudbury sent a card in the mail.

In its Veda wrote: "In such a short time you arrived at the top, CONGRATULATIONS!"

That's a strange message she thought. Carol hadn't considered at all that this new job was anything more than the next step. All that she was concerned about at this time was getting Mikelle through college. She just wanted to earn enough to pay the bills and put some money away for a retirement. That morning, before she met with the chairman, she thought about where she was going.

Sick Kids is the affectionate name that everyone uses for The Hospital for Sick Children. It is an institution founded in 1875 when Toronto was a growing city of sixty-thousand inhabitants. Today it serves the entire fifteen million Ontario residents and patients the world over. If there was a pinnacle of charitable institutions to serve in Canada, then Sick Kids would be it. Carol had reached the top of her profession and didn't realize it.

Breaking the news of her leaving to the Board was not easy. It had been four years of unprecedented success for their foundation. Carol felt that she was leaving them on a very solid financial footing. They had to try to keep her.

"We'll pay you whatever they do, even more if you want." They offered.

"It's not the money." Carol stated. "The campaign is an enormous challenge."

"We could get more staff for you, new offices if you'd like," he said.

Carol assured him that her mind was made up and there was no turning back. The compliment of being wanted for this prestigious position was so rewarding. Sick Kids was eager for her to start too, they wanted her right away. She recommended Alicia to the board to assume the CEO position and they agreed. Carol then spent the next two weeks working with her and preparing Alicia to take over.

In the end the board had a nice dinner party for Carol's farewell. They presented her with an engraved silver business card holder that she used thereafter. In her words of thanks to the board that night she made sure that they knew Alicia was ready. The point was not only to assure the board but also to assure Alicia's willingness to move up.

The hospital had acquired an entire floor of offices in an adjacent building to house the new research foundation. Carol again would be the Chief Executive Officer. There was an existing small staff at the hospital for fundraising that was not involved in

Carol's campaign yet. When she walked into the offices that first morning it was completely empty. Not a stick of furniture or even a phone. They gave her six months to get the campaign up and running and she would need every day of it.

Using a budget established for her of hospital resources she first bought furniture and office equipment and a phone system. The process of hiring staff began and was the segment that Carol spent the most time on. When questioned by the board about her thoroughness in interviews she explains her need for just the right fit. She didn't want to be wasting time trying someone out and letting them go if they didn't work out.

Selecting a computing and software system would be an obstacle. They would need software for both fundraising and research. Not something that Carol knew much about, she relied on the usual deep research. Interviewing a number of companies there was one firm that invited her to their offices in Indiana. They sent a limousine from the airport to a great hotel. Power lunches and fancy dinners followed, the whole executive treatment. Thinking back to her humble roots on the farm, how did she get here. This was a new experience that she thoroughly enjoyed.

Before the six months were up Carol had assembled all of the offices into place. Staff was assembled into three main divisions. The Major Gifts staff were the people taking the message into the community. Major Gift individuals were very hard to find, the outgoing types that could ask the wealthy to give to their capacity. Many interviews would prove a candidate did not have the combination of intelligence and manner to ask appropriately. A Major Gifts staffer had to be able to take criticism and respond to negative reactions. Those that Carol selected were very bright, experienced, and confident. The qualities that were required in them would prove to her that they could be hard to manage. Carol was their leader and the chief Major Gift collector.

The Research staff did the collecting of data relating to contact information and sources of funding. Carol again showed them the hard work and methods that had always worked for her. The researchers were also involved with the asking for major gifts. They would often accompany Carol and the others on appointments with potential donors.

The third division would be the Events staff. Not one of Carols favorite aspects of the fundraising work, it is a necessary function to promote awareness. The planning and carrying out of these events in the community can be a lot of work for smaller monetary returns. Carol was the voice for the hospital at many of the events. She provided the keynote speeches to the patrons attending events that identified the good works they would be donating to.

After some time into the campaign the major gifts were coming in, events were happening, and the goal was in sight. Carol was approached by one of the board of directors about hiring a major gifts staffer. He was a young man with an advanced degree in business and came with his own staff of two researchers. After a brief interview she reluctantly took them on. With the memory of her successful hiring of Alicia at the past job, she decided to give it a try. Carol set them to work at learning a presentation that she had developed. Once learned and adapted they could set up appointments with potentially big donors.

The day came that this new staffer came to Carol in a panic. He appeared in her office in a stained old shirt and tie. Wrinkled pants and shoes that were broken at the soles. His unkempt hair topped off the sight.

"Carol, I have an appointment with an executive on Bay Street and I'm afraid. I can't remember the script and I might blow it."

"You aren't ready for this. Cancel the appointment." She demanded.

She first instructed him that if not prepared with his approach, then he should not be making appointments. Next, she took apart his appearance piece by piece. Explaining that his dress and grooming had no place in her office let alone in the presence of a major donor. This MBA had very little idea of what she was getting at. He told her that his clothes were fine, he wore them everywhere.

Carol had always been careful to dress and appear professional. Not extravagant, she had just six business outfits and wore them in rotation. They were the same suits that she had made years ago at her shop in Blind River. Her clothes were well made by her hands of quality fabric. Scarves and accessories would change the look frequently.

"If you can't spend some of the money that we pay you for a decent wardrobe and haircut we are going to have a problem." She concluded sending him away to cancel the appointment.

Later Carol did try to help this young man by pointing out other men in the office that he should emulate. She suggested some stores that would help him. Working with him when she could, it just wasn't getting through.

"I have a Master's Degree in Business Administration. I should know what I'm doing more so than you." He told Carol at one point. She gave up on him then and let things take their course.

The young man began making appointments with some important potential donors. After his first failure Carol started following up with the men and women that he had met with. There were four more failures at appointments that followed. Carol received poor reviews of his approach and abilities from every one of her follow up calls.

Since they came in as a team, she called the three of them into her office and terminated them on the spot. It was something that she had never wanted to do in her leadership role, and she didn't want to do it again. The director that had recommended the man to her came and asked what had gone wrong.

"He's a very smart guy. You're going to have to explain why you did this," he said.

"They were holding us back," she continued, "He failed on five meetings with donors that I know would have given a big gift. In fact, I followed up after each one of his meetings and I got a significant pledge from three of them."

There was very little questioning of Carol's methods from the board of directors after that. Besides, the money was pouring in and the goal looked to be easily within reach. Easily would be the wrong way to describe it. The attaining of that goal was coming from the hard work of the staff and led by example from Carol. In spite of this one individual, Carol was well liked by all of the foundation staff. There was very little turnover and there was never a need for termination again.

Along with leading the huge research fundraising campaign Carol was appointed one of five members of a Senior Management Team for the Hospital. It added another layer of work demands and preparation. This was a tough group and Carol proved her management ability well. She was always ready with a detailed report to the team of the campaign's progress. It also involved her into the decision making for overall hospital policies. Carol became good friends with Sue on this team. Sue was a trusted colleague that Carol could go to in confidence for advice and support.

There was very little time for a social life. The demands of the campaign required many twelve hour days. Monday through Friday she would be up at 5:30 AM, shower, breakfast and at her desk by seven. Somewhere between seven and eight PM she left for home, ate a light meal, and went to bed. She also worked to a lesser degree on Saturdays and Sundays. The positive results for the hospital reflected this dedication.

There was one morning that Carol got a message from a woman on the hospital staff that she didn't know. The woman worked as a receptionist part time and had nothing at all to do with the fundraising. She asked if Carol would have coffee with her some morning. Carol agreed and they met soon after. She told Carol that she was back in Toronto caring for her mother who was ill. Previous to coming home she worked for Disney Studios in their Art Department. She presented Carol with a framed painting she had created and explained that the gift was because she admired Carol so much. The beautiful floral artwork has since hung in an honored place at all of Carol's homes.

She did have some acquaintances, mostly involved in the arts community. She had not dated at all since the divorce . She was working at her office late and remembered Ann's call from yesterday. Ann was a gallery owner and had invited her to a show opening that evening. She had missed one opening, maybe two before and decided to close up the office and go to this one.

Tired as usual, Carol planned to stay maybe an hour. After having a sparkling water poured in a wine glass, she made the rounds taking in the art. She made sure to speak to Ann wanting her to know that she was there. Entering one of the gallery rooms she met a man who introduced himself quite graciously. He was very well dressed and well spoken. It was obvious that he was a successful man. Carol made small talk with him, telling him what she did for the hospital. He explained that he was at the show with a date who was off chatting with a group of their friends. Saying that he should be getting back, he asked for Carol's phone number. Thinking that he may be a potential donor she gave him her card.

He called the next morning. After a brief conversation he ask her out to dinner that night. Mentioning the name of a very fine restaurant as one of his favorites, Carol was intrigued but wary. *'What about the woman he was with at the gallery?'* she thought. She put him off with the fact that it was a very busy time for her. She had too many events planned in the course of the campaign for Sick Kids. Maybe another time might be better she said being vague. Carol was interested in him but truly was busy with the campaign. Saying goodbye and hanging up the phone, she wondered if she would ever hear from him again.

He called again two days later. They talked for a bit getting to know each other superficially. His outgoing personality was starting to become attractive to her. He again suggested dinner, this time he offered that she could name the date. Carol got his phone number and promised to call back in a day or so.

Her daughter was off between semesters and staying at the apartment. Carol told Mikelle about the man she had met and his persistent calls.

"Mom, you have to go out with him!" Mikelle was adamant. "You need to get out and enjoy yourself. You're working too hard."

Mikelle was right of course. The campaign was in high gear now and working with a momentum of its own. It was time for Carol to ease off a bit and enjoy the fruits of her hard work. She called Ron that night and made plans to meet him at his favorite restaurant.

Ron was there waiting at their table, an iced Johnny Walker Red in front of him. Carol ordered her one cocktail for the evening. They talked for an hour as if there was no one else in the room. Finally, a meal was ordered with Ron suggesting the house specialty. Carol enjoyed the meal and Ron's company immensely. Before she knew it, she noticed the busy restaurant had cleared out. They had been talking for four hours and it was after midnight. Ron asked if she would like to continue the conversation at his apartment. Carol laughed, she thanked him for the evening and left on her own.

Needless to say, the next day at the office was a blur. Carol had taken that rare chance to let go and enjoy herself. The exhaustion would pass but the memory of Ron was fresh in her mind. She hoped that he was impressed too. Would he call again? She certainly hoped so.

The campaign was coming to an end and the seemingly unattainable goal was imminent. It seemed unreal that they had actually raised a billion dollars for the research endowment at Sick Kids hospital. It was through pledges from major donors of millions. It came from events that took days of planning and capital outlays to bring in small profits from all over the province. It came from families whose lives were affected by childhood illness. It came from people who cared about their neighbors and friends and family. Carol learned how to tap into that community and how to make it a reality.

DOROTHY

Ron continued to call after their first date, but Carol's time and effort was focused on the campaign. He was persistent though and they did see each other more as the year went by. She became quite attracted to the confidence and accomplishment that Ron exuded. His position as a partner at the investment banking firm introduced her to his many friends in the industry. At one point Carol told him that if they were going to date exclusively, he would have to make a substantial gift to the campaign. He did that right away.

Since she left Blind River Carol had always taken her vacations back home. At first it was because she missed Mikelle so much. Once Mikelle joined her in the city they would return north for Andre. She would spend the week helping him with the house, cooking for the freezer and visiting family. Once she and Andre were divorced there wasn't any more need to visit Blind River. Her mother had also relocated to southern Ontario. Most of the Aunts, Uncles and cousins had also left there.

They were now dating each other exclusively and Ron would ask Carol to come live with him at his apartment. She always turned him down, so he asked her to join him on a trip to Italy. She had six weeks of vacation time to use so they planned for a twenty day trip. Flying from Toronto directly to Florence, Ron rented a car at the airport for the drive to the hotel. Carol knew that Ron wasn't a very good driver, now she learned that he couldn't drive a standard transmission either. Grinding the gears and lurching Ron got the car moving forward at a very slow pace. He couldn't get the car into a higher gear and the horns were blaring and drivers shouting Italian curses at them as they puttered along.

"We need to stop and get some help" Carol pleaded.

"Don't worry sweetheart, They can go around us" Ron said.

Finally, Ron got the car stopped in front of a store. Carol was going to ask for directions.

"You can't speak Italian darling," he said.

"I'll take care of it," she said. Carol was able to get directions to the hotel just a short distance away. During a campaign for the Hearing Foundation, it was required that she learn the American Sign Language. It helped to translate their need in Italian.

Once back in the car and more gear grinding, Ron couldn't get the car into reverse. Carol took over the driving from then on. Ron was fine with just enjoying the ride. At the hotel Carol had the car changed to an automatic. From Florence she drove the Autostrada to Umbria in terror at a hundred and thirty kilometers per hour (80 mph). Again, the Italian drivers were cursing their slow pace.

Despite the driving they had a great time and Carol was thrilled with her first trip abroad. There would be many more to come for the couple. Back in Canada they both settled back into work. As the campaign for research was moving toward the goal they had fallen in love and Ron asked her to marry him. Carol put off an answer for some time. She was unsure and wanted to know Ron better.

Ron would ask every chance he got. "Have you got an answer to my question yet?"

That winter Ron asked if Carol and Mikelle would join him in Naples, Florida for the Christmas season. It would be the first time in Florida for her and she found it to be boring. The weather was cool and all there was to do was eat and drink. Ron promised that he would pay for everything and that was the case. He proved to be very generous the entire time that she knew him.

The Senior Management Team that Carol was part of had decided that Carol's position was to be extended beyond her current contract. The hospital would make CEO of Development a permanent position and Carol would be in line for a substantial raise in pay. Along with that would come more benefits and responsibility. It was to be a gratifying reward for the effort that she had put in. When she started it seemed impossible that they could raise a billion dollars, but it became for her, a campaign that could not fail.

It was soon after the trip to Florida that Carol relented and agreed to marry Ron. The condo where he lived downtown was convenient to Carol's office, but she felt it was not suitable for two married people. She insisted that they buy a home. Carol found a house that she liked on Spadina Avenue not too far from downtown. Ron gave her the credit card and carte blanche to decorate any way she wanted. Ron insisted the backyard be beautifully landscaped and had the basement made into an apartment for Mikelle. Of course, Mikelle's apartment was finished as well as the other floors.

Carol's wedding dress was being made by an upscale couture shop in Yorkville. At the measuring Carol had told the shop owner exactly what she wanted. It was a week before the wedding when Carol and the wedding planner went to pick up the dress. When she tried on the dress the disappointment took some time to comprehend. She had spent a large amount for it.

Finally, Carol said to the shop owner: "I can't wear this. It looks like an amateur sewed it."

The owner was mortified. "I'll just write you a check for your deposit," she said.

"Yes, I think you should." The shop owner was mad and took the check with resentment.

Leaving the shop, she had no idea what to do. With just a week until the wedding she felt panic. They walked toward the car and noticed another shop sign for a wedding designer. Entering the store Carol told the man, who turned out to be the designer, that she needed a wedding dress for August 28.

"Is that one year from now or two?" He asked.

"It's next week." Carol replied. "Have you got something on the rack we can buy?"

He was stunned but exclaimed. "A beautiful woman like you can't be married in a dress off the rack."

"Are you the man for the job?" Carol asked and he was. The design that he put together in a week was what she wanted and expertly made.

The wedding was planned as an outdoor event that summer at Ron's country home near Guelph. The altar was set up by the lake, two stone stairways below the main house. The guests sat on a large lawn and a string quartet played as the wedding party descended the stairs. Ron's son guided Carol down and gave her away. It was a perfect day for both the weather and the ceremony. The huge crowd at the reception included all of Carol and Ron's family and friends for a great party.

Mikelle was Maid of Honor and her speech was perfection. "When you have a mother as special as mine you become very protective." She then declared that Ron had gained her trust.

After the wedding Carol and Ron settled into the house on Spadina and Carol went back to work on the campaign. Ron's firm had established a mandatory retirement age at sixty and that day was coming soon. He and Carol were discussing his retirement when he surprised her with a request.

"Would you retire with me?" He asked. "Would you resign from Sick Kids?"

Carol had no notion that she could stop working. She is younger than Ron and was not ready personally or financially to retire. Besides that, she was up for a big raise.

"I have enough for us to live well for a hundred years." "You don't need to be working this hard anymore" He promised.

"I'll have to think about that for a long time." She told him but the thought of leaving the workforce began to enter her mind.

Over the next few days, they discussed the situation, and it became apparent to Carol that she could agree to Ron's request. The idea of a more carefree life of travel and art seemed wonderful now to her. Ron retired from the firm and Carol put in her resignation soon after.

During this time Carol had been trying to reach her old and close friend Dorothy. She would call her cell phone and leave messages that were never returned. It bothered Carol at first and then she became concerned. Eventually she called Dorothy's home phone number and spoke to Eric, her husband. Eric couldn't understand why Carol's calls weren't being answered. Dorothy said nothing to him about it.

"I'll talk to her and have her call you." Eric said.

Dorothy was still working in sales then but not traveling like she did when Carol first met her. When Carol moved from Blind River to the city, they were her only friends for some time. Carol would stay at their home in Toronto when she visited from Whitby. They stayed very close when Carol moved to Toronto also. When Dorothy eventually called, they decided to meet for lunch at a familiar place.

Their conversation was like it had always been, warm and friendly. They caught up on all that was new. Carol didn't mention that Dorothy and Eric didn't come to her wedding despite the invitation. Dorothy didn't say why it was that she ignored Carol's calls. After lunch Dorothy's tone changed dramatically.

"We can't see each other anymore after this." Dorothy said. The words didn't make sense to Carol.

"What's wrong? Is there a problem I can help with?" Carol wanted to know.

"Rich people and poor people can't be friends." Dorothy said it matter of factly.

Carol tried to reason with Dorothy that nothing had changed. She was still the same person and true to her roots. Dorothy would not be swayed. She got up, said goodbye and walked out. Carol would never see her or talk to her again. It was Dorothy's choice; Carol was deeply saddened.

It was only a matter of days after his retirement that Ron grew restless and had to go back to work. He had no other interests or hobbies other than investing. Working from an office at home he still dealt with his associates from the old firm. They had more time now for travel and relaxation, but Ron's work was intruding more as time went on. The days that he spent away at long lunches downtown were sometimes lonely for Carol. Ron would also take trips to the West coast for a couple of days of business. At one point he informed Carol that the company wanted him to spend two weeks a month in Vancouver.

The idea that he was needed to be in Vancouver was hard to believe. It was even harder to accept when Ron said that he didn't want Carol to travel with him. She was suspicious but accepted the situation for now. Carol came to the decision that she would start her own business now. With Ron away and working then she would need to fill the void in her life too. The pace that she had been working at Sick Kids would make separation from a career difficult. She made a promise to herself that she would only work four days a week and stuck to it.

Ethier & Associates was the company that she formed in an office rented in Yorkville. Carol had become well known throughout the fundraising business in Toronto. She used the contacts developed over the years of successful campaigns to advertise by word of mouth. Calls were made to Board directors, CEO men and women and soon she was inundated by calls for consulting services. The business plan was to provide feasibility studies to the CEOs of foundations and their boards. The goal was to provide coaching and leadership training to development directors of campaigns that were lagging.

Not wanting to expand the business beyond herself, Carol found that she had to turn down a lot of potential clients. She had the benefit of choosing a desirable client that paid well. Her first client was the Ontario Society for the Prevention of Cruelty to Animals. A strange choice since she really didn't care for dogs and cats. Maybe it was the love that she had for the animals on the farm from her childhood. The fear she had for dogs goes back to Kynoch too. The neighbors' dogs snarling and biting them as they walked to school. She took the OSPCA job because it was a big challenge. The goal was to raise their sights.

Her first day at the foundation they gave Carol an office to work out of. The staff there was encouraged to bring their pets to work and Carol was apprehensive of the dogs. She had brought a leather briefcase to work, and her lunch was inside. A huge dog lumbered into her office and put his massive head on the desk near her hand. Carol was terrified and couldn't move. Obviously smelling the food, the dog grabbed her briefcase and took off down the hall. Carol gave chase and finally cornered the dog in the break room. Grabbing her case, she fought a tug of war with the snarling dog. She ripped it out of his teeth and slammed a door closed before it could follow her. She continued to use the briefcase with the tooth marks but never brought her lunch in again.

GLEN EDYTH

As it turned out the choice for the home on Spadina Avenue didn't work. It was a busy noisy street that concerned Carol. Every time that Ron left in his Jeep it seemed that he would back into the street without looking. After a year of living with that Carol plied Ron with the idea of moving to a better neighborhood. With the help of Ron's personal assistant, David, they began looking at properties. A place was found on a quiet cul-de-sac near the Spadina house at Glen Edyth Drive. A very upscale neighborhood of large homes that were a little older, This house needed some considerable updating so Carol set to work in the selecting of contractors that she could trust. She picked out every new fixture and all of the materials down to the nails. Working closely with all of the craftsmen Carol was learning a lot about renovations.

Her work also continued with Ethier & Associates, she had four main clients under contract. Besides the client work Carol was also being contracted for speaking engagements to foundations and one day seminars. It came to a point that she needed some help with organizing and preparation. She thought about Kim and the great help she had been at a previous employer. On a whim she called her.

"Hello Kim, this is Carol Ethier, how have you been." Carol said, Kim was happy to hear from her. She told Carol that life was good, but the law firm was only giving her one day a week of employment. Her music and performance work weren't paying the bills either.

"Would you like to work for me two or three days a week?" Carol asked and Kim jumped at the chance.

They set up their offices in a remodeled area in the basement of the house on Glen Edyth. Working with their desks facing in an L pattern the two were soon an efficient team.

Carol would walk the neighborhood most days for exercise and fresh air. The surrounding area was bordered by parks and the historic grounds of the Casa Loma mansion. Frequently on her walks she would see an elderly lady walking her two large dogs. Always alone this woman lived in the largest mansion on the street. Carol would smile and wave, sometimes say hello, but the greeting was never returned. Instead, what she got was a scowl or totally ignored. It was unnerving but she tried not to let it bother her.

One day Carol planned to talk to the lady. She walked up the long walkway to the front door and rang the bell. The big dogs barked behind the door before it opened a little more than a crack. The elderly woman shouted: "May I help you?" And quieted the dogs.

Carol responded: "Hello, I'm Carol Ethier and I live in the house at the corner there."

She said it and pointed to her left, three houses away. The door opened a little more and the woman behind it came into view. She introduced herself and informed Carol that she doesn't take visitors since her husband had passed away.

"I'm working with the Society for the Prevention of Cruelty to Animals, the SPCA." "I'm wondering if you would consider giving a donation to our cause." With that the door opened wider and Carol was invited in. "It's my favorite charity." The widow said. Entering into the foyer, Carol froze as the two dogs circled her. The irritable woman didn't invite her any further into the house. Carol stood there and talked about the needs of the defenseless animals and the costs of providing shelter to them.

Cutting her off the woman snapped: "I suppose that you're looking for ten or twenty dollars." Her manner was not getting any friendlier.

"No actually we believe that your gift could be as much as one million dollars." Carol replied. Carol looked her firmly in the eye. She was well practiced in asking for a major gift.

The woman sputtered out a few words before asking how Carol had arrived at such an outrageous amount of money to ask for. Carol explained that the foundation had done research and had software that they used to determine a donor's giving capacity. The fact was that Carol's new firm did not have the staff or the software that she used in previous campaigns. The one million dollar request was made up in her mind as she stood in the foyer. Carol knew from her years of experience that if you start high and fail, you are still up there to bring in a large donation.

"I'm going to have to think about it" the woman said hoping to end this conversation now.

"I'll come back in a week then." Carol said.

"Make it two weeks." The woman demanded

Carol took care to write down a time and date that she could come back to discuss the gift.

On the appointed day Carol returned to the big house. After ringing the bell, she could hear the dogs barking behind the door. The widow did not answer the door, so Carol left planning to come back later. When she returned in the afternoon there was no answer at the door again. The next day went by without Carol seeing the woman at all. She didn't see her walking the dogs or driving away from the house. It was three days later that Carol saw the woman in her yard. She prepared herself and walked over to confront the woman.

"You don't give up easily, do you?" The woman sounded as if she was bothered.

"If I gave up then the poor animals would have no help and would suffer a terrible fate." Carol didn't really have the same kind of empathy for the animals that she did for the children that were cared for at Sick Kids Hospital. But she did care deeply for the cause and the people that worked for it. She made her plea all over again and the woman invited Carol into the house to discuss the gift. At the dining room table, the two worked out an arrangement that would fund a pledge of five hundred thousand dollars pledge paid over four consecutive years. The woman signed the pledge, Carol thanked her in a business-like manner and left.

Carol and Ron's married life together had become a whirlwind of activity. Both were working and Carol would concentrate on her business most when Ron was away to the West coast of Canada. Ron was splitting his time now between Vancouver and Toronto. When he was home in Toronto there would be a succession of dining out and parties at the Glen Edyth house. They had a large group of friends and business associates and were never lacking for a social gathering. Besides that, the couple took numerous vacation trips to Europe and the United States. To escape the winters there would be trips to Florida for weeks at a time.

Ron would call almost every night from his business trips in Vancouver. Carol asked many times if she could fly out and meet him there.

"You'd hate it here; it is a lousy city." He would say. "I hate it here."

Ron would suggest that they meet in San Francisco or Las Vegas or some other fun city. He would send Carol the tickets and they had great times with Ron generously covering tours and fine dining. He showered Carol with expensive gifts of jewelry, designer outfits and such. Carol was very much in love and extremely happy. But some doubts were creeping in.

The time with Ron seemed to fly by and now eight years into their marriage Carol got an unsolicited offer. A man that Carol had never met called and wanted to buy her company. He currently owned a marketing company and told Carol that he felt the fundraising business could make him more money. Carol was reluctant given that he had no experience, and she was protective of her clients.

The thought of being free of work again was alluring though. There could be more time for travel and exploring her affection for art, music, stage, and theatre. And best of all time for social life with Ron and friends. The monetary offer was much more than she expected but there were concerns. The man explained that the name Ethier & Associates would remain on the company. He said that the reputation that Carol had established in the industry was the most important asset. She could stay on as an advisor if she wanted. This man's company had a staff, but they had never worked in the fundraising industry before.

In the end Carol decided to sell but for a slightly lower amount. She demanded that her name was no longer to be associated with the new company. She would turn over all of her contacts and clients and leave the company. She still had concerns that her good name may be negatively affected by this change. As if to prove her hesitance, soon after the new company did fail.

She was free from work now and did take advantage of all of those things she had been wanting to do. Ron's generosity only increased, and he suggested that Carol travel with friends and get away as much as she could. Mikelle was studying for an advanced degree now and living in Paris. Carol made a number of trips there alone and with her good friend Patty.

Through a good friend she learned about a man that could help answer her reservations about Ron. She made the very difficult decision to hire the man, a private investigator. What she learned from the PI was devastating. There was another woman in Vancouver and Ron had been unfaithful in Toronto.

As usual in a crisis, Carol called her daughter, Mikelle was at the house just minutes later. Carol told her all that she had learned about Ron and the women. Mikelle was very protective of her mom. She could see that her mother was deeply hurt from the betrayal.

They proceeded to confront Ron with all of the information that the investigator had given them. The blame fell strictly on him for all of the pain they were feeling. After the point was driven home that he had demolished Carol's trust and love it was concluded that Ron should leave.

Ron called the next morning and continued to call over the ensuing days. Carol listened to his pleas of how sorry he was and that he would change. She was having none of it. The hurt that she felt was deep and devastating. She refused to let him back and only agreed to let his friend come to the house for his clothes and accessories. It took months of her mourning the loss of her love until she finally agreed to meet him for lunch. They met downtown at his usual place, nearby was an apartment that he had rented.

Ron implored her to take him back. He said he could change his ways. The Vancouver trips and relationship were over. He would stop working, if he ever really were, and they would travel. He promised her that if she would let him come home that he would devote himself to making her happy. After putting up with his dialog for an hour she told him that she would consider it and give him an answer in a week.

"Don't call me while I'm thinking about this. I'll call you in a week if the answer is yes." Carol said as she got up and left Ron sitting at the table.

Ron's usual tactic of gifts and flowers delivered to the Glen Edyth house followed every day for the week. Carol spent the time with Mikelle consoling and discussing Ron's possible return. Mikelle was against the idea. She knew that the hurt of Ron's betrayal had inflicted much pain on her mother. She resented him for it and felt he had to pay the emotional price too. Carol was softening though and against her better judgement she decided to accept Ron back. She called him on the appointed day.

"Give it a couple of days" She said. "You can come back on Friday"

Carol knew that it was a mistake from the first day of Ron's return. He was overly attentive, and they returned to the usual social course of dining out sometimes alone or with friends. Ron was his usual outgoing and happy self. Carol though was a shell of her former self, emotionally she felt empty. She tried to regain her feelings for Ron as he tried to convince her that he was changing. The first time that he left the house alone he said to meet a friend for lunch. Carol new then that she could never trust Ron again.

At a moment when Carol felt that Ron could fully understand what she was asking, they spoke earnestly to each other.

"Ron, I want you to be perfectly honest with me. You can't change and be faithful to me, can you?" Carol's question was softly spoken but had the weight of finality.

"No darling, I could not promise you that" Ron's truthful answer was what she expected.

Carol planned with legal counsel and prepared for the divorce. Her sadness grew as they planned for the dissolution of the marriage. Carol felt that Ron had taken her from a lucrative career, and she wanted to be compensated for the missed years of high earning. To Ron's credit he agreed with all that she asked for and has always lived up to their agreement.

BEAR'S PAW

A year had now past since the marriage with Ron had ended, Carol was finally feeling herself again. The time had been a struggle to overcome the profound depression that overwhelmed her. With the help of her daughter and good friends like Patty she was able to take advantage of what was rightfully hers. Ron was equally supportive through it all. The house on Glen Edyth had been sold now, a bittersweet memory. Carol had made sure to have most of the furnishings that she had designed for transferred to her new condo.

It was at this point that Carol made an appointment to see her financial planner. The years with Ron were very comfortable but now she would need to take care of her own affairs, Entering the downtown offices of the Royal Bank of Canada at the appointed time they met and went over Carol's situation to her satisfaction. At this juncture entering retirement years her financial status was healthy. It was at this meeting that her advisor called his second in command on intercom.

"Susan, could you come in here a moment. I'd like for you to meet an important client of ours." He spoke into the phone. He was smiling as their eyes met across his desk.

Carol, as was always her style was dressed impeccably for business. Her hair and makeup done well and demeanor professional.

Susan entered the office after just seconds and introductions were made. The advisor made sure that his top assistant knew that when Carol Ethier was to call, she would to be given the utmost of attention. It seemed to Carol that he was intentionally showing Susan what a polished professional appearance Carol presented. Carol couldn't help but notice that Susan was a fine looking young woman but was certainly lacking in style and comportment. Her hair straight and drab brown, minimal if any makeup and her clothes and shoes looked plain and somewhat worn. She made her exit as Carol and the planner were wrapping up the meeting. He promised another appointment in a month to update her on the transfer of some assets.

Leaving the bank building an idea was formulating in Carol's mind. She couldn't stop thinking about Susan and the plight that she appeared to be in. The young woman seemed to be quite bright but showed outwardly to be forlorn and sad. Carol imagined that Susan felt she had no future in banking.

The next appointment that Carol had with her banker came a month later. They went over Carol's position and all seemed to be in order. Toward the end of their conversation, she brought up her idea.

"I have decided to open a new business." Carol stated. "It involves Personal Image Consulting. I hope to be attracting clients that may need help with enhancing aspects of their career."

"That is a great idea." He answered. "You do present an impressive image yourself."

Carol went on to describe the kinds of services that she would be providing. She told the banker that she would be setting up an office in her condo. A brochure was being crafted and she would get one to him when it was done. She gave him the business card she had created.

"I have your first client in mind right now." He told her. "I had hoped when I introduced you to Susan that she could see what a professional image you presented."

He spoke vividly about Susan's brilliance and business acumen. This manager knew that Susan was capable of great things at the bank. There was something holding her back, a lack of confidence in herself. It showed outward in her appearance and comportment.

"Susan will be having her review this week and we are going to be discussing your services." He informed her. "You should be expecting a call from her right after."

Carol took Susan on as a client and immediately began the process. They went shopping together with Carol showing her the shops that featured what she knew to be fashionable business attire. From a new wardrobe down to the shoes and even what jewelry to wear the transformation taking place was lifting Susan's spirit. Next, they made extended appointments at the salon that Carol used. Susan's hair was cut to a style and flair that complimented her. They met with a makeup artist that brought out the beauty and confidence Susan had beneath. After this period of makeover along with some encouraging discussions on office deportment, Susan was ready. She had no qualms about paying the fee as Susan knew that the job Carol had done was excellent.

The life changing conversion that Carol had helped Susan obtain didn't go unnoticed at the bank and their clientele. She soon had a flood of requests for her services. She became most particular with whom she would take on as a client. Not wanting to expand the business beyond herself, Carol turned down many more requests than she accepted. Susan was soon promoted at the bank; her former manager couldn't have been happier for her. The bank had even requested that Carol prepare a day long presentation to a large group of managerial candidates. At the end of the seminar Carol offered a question and answer period. One young man's question is memorable to her.

He stood and asked: " I've been wanting to cut and color my hair into a Mohawk. Do you think that could affect my position with RBC?" Carol's answer brought out roaring laughs and applause.

"If your goal is to end your employment with the bank, it's your choice." She said as the meeting came to an end.

The capacity to be able to choose her clients carefully was a luxury earned from a successful career and prudent investment. She was able to say no to the braggarts or selfish that requested her help. There was one man that came to her with a story that intrigued her. It was the kind of project that she desired. He explained that he was most successful at selling real estate and had a prolific specialty for single family homes.

"I want to change my focus to selling high end properties to more wealthy clients". He explained. "In other words, I want to step up my game"

It was the kind of project that whetted Carol's interest. It was the challenge, not the money that interested her. Her years of experience in fundraising had trained her in just how to approach an affluent client.

She took him on and began by saying: "Let's start by having a detailed inspection of your closet." The man stood by while Carol when through each article and picked off most of the hangers.

"You can't be seen in any of these outfits if you want to succeed with your target clients." Carol referred the young man to a shop that she knew the Bay Street directors used. "You have to spend money to make money the old saying goes."

This young man followed Carol's advice and went on to create an impressive portfolio of sales in downtown Toronto condominiums. He was most grateful, even asking her to a party that friends were having for him. She and her daughter went to the party and graciously left early after experiencing the scene. A naked model lying on the dining room table covered by snacks. The heavy smell of marijuana hung in the air.

Her clients came to her in different ways. Once while waiting in a doctor's office for an appointment, she had a conversion with the receptionist. She told the woman about the business that she had started.

"Could you help my daughter?" The receptionist asked "She's just taken a job with the Mayor's office in Chicago. She's extremely nervous about it. We've heard Mayor Daly can be tough."

Every time that Carol saw that doctor his receptionist would update Carol with how well the daughter was doing in her career. Personal references are what enhance a successful business. Carol's business thrived on them. Good recommendations travel fast through the community and Carol's reputation for positive results was established. It was almost two years now since Carol started the image consulting business. She was again approached by a man that wanted to buy her business. He said that he would want her name to remain on the business.

"I don't think so." She answered him. "The business is so new and it's doing so well. I'm not ready to give it up yet."

Carol lied. She was thinking more than ever now about retirement. The work was getting exhausting and her ability for freedom to enjoy life was hampered. In fact, when the offer came to sell, Carol was having a working vacation of a month in Florida. With her good friend Shirley, they were having a sunny and warm retreat from the cold damp Toronto winter. Carol told the man that she would have an answer for him when she returned.

One day during the vacation Shirley suggested that they look at real estate listings. She had picked up a brochure that showed open houses going on that day. One of the first places that they looked at was a condominium in a golf community called Bear's Paw. It is one of many designed and endorsed by the golf legend Jack Nicklaus. His nickname, The Golden Bear, graced many of his designed communities.

Carol loved the home; it was decorated in French Provincial colors and furnishings that she favored. The realtor pressed Carol hard to make an offer. She explained that the previous owners, a married couple, had passed away and their family was selling. The real estate market was hot in Naples at that time and Carol was in no way looking to buy in Florida. The idea hadn't crossed her mind, they were just wanting something to amuse themselves. Carol put down a ridiculously low offer.

"I couldn't give the sellers this price." The realtor said. "It's too embarrassing."

"That's what I can afford. It's my final offer" Carol replied, the offer was almost half the listed price. She and Shirley left, and Carol didn't think any more about it, assuming that the realtor wouldn't submit the offer.

Later that evening they were having a cocktail before dinner when a call came into Carol's cell phone. The caller started by saying: "Congratulations, you bought property in Florida!" It wasn't planned but Carol was thrilled. Especially that the price was far below the market value. She and Shirley celebrated then started to prepare for their return to Toronto . The vacation was coming to an end.

The closing of the condo sale was slightly more complicated by the distance and cross border transactions, but it got done in a short time. In the meantime, Carol called back to the man who had offered to buy her business. As was the case with her previous business Carol was reluctant to leave her name on a company that she didn't control. She told him that it was just not possible. He insisted that the value of the company was all in her name.

"You can name your price." He stated. "I will pay whatever you want."

The thought of making a substantial profit was tempting but Carol's name was too valuable to her. She had no intention of starting up another company. She agreed to take a lower price for the company without her name. She did turn over all of her contacts and methods to the new owner this time. She did know that he did make a success of the business that she created.

Carol felt truly free now with no career to occupy her. She took time to spend a lot of time with friends in pursuing her interest in the arts. She attended concerts, opera, plays, movies. Toured art galleries and began to dabble in painting herself. She planned to fly to Florida and take physical possession of her condominium. The realtor had mailed keys, and ownership papers and she was eager to see what she owned.

The plane from Toronto landed at Fort Myers late in the evening. When she cleared the car rental counter and drove away from the airport it was already dark. She had no idea where she was going but just pointed the car towards Naples. By some twist of fate, she took the second Naples exit at Golden Gate parkway and a few blocks towards the city a sign pointed to Bears Paw. After a stop at the gate, the guard gave her directions to her unit, a short drive into the community.

After a good night's sleep Carol woke up to a clear and warm sunny morning on her veranda overlooking the eighteenth hole of the beautiful golf course. An osprey dove from its nest onto the pond and grabbed a fish for its breakfast. She was home, a new home in the beauty and calm of Southwest Florida.

NIAGARA

Carol would continue to split her time between Toronto and Naples for a time. She easily made new friends in the Bears Paw community during the busy winter season. A relationship would develop that would result in Carol's obtaining permanent resident status in the United States. Taking advantage of the hot real estate markets, Carol would be able to profit from the sale of her condominiums in both Toronto and Naples. The couple would combine to buy a house in a different community nearby in Naples. New friends were made and those made at Bear's Paw remained close. She was becoming more acclimated to life in Florida, even learning to enjoy golf. The visits to Canada would become fewer since her daughters move to western Canada. Mikelle and Aaron would visit her in Naples.

Carol's relationship was to end suddenly. Again, needing to move onward Carol found a great deal on a coach home in the gated community of Grey Oaks. Dear friends that she had made at Bear's Paw had moved there and recommended it. She proceeded to redecorate the Grey Oaks property with style and grace. Not quite a year at that property the market for real estate in Naples convinced her that a healthy profit could be made in selling. The Grey Oaks property sold almost immediately. Carol saw the property as an opportunity to raise US dollars.

There were many new communities developing in Naples at that time and Carol chose The Isles to build a new single family house from scratch. After picking out just the right lot to locate on, meetings with builder and architect started. The lot had to have a water view, as did most of her homes going back to Toronto and even Blind River. The calming effect of a water view from home was relieving for her.

Carol selected just the right design that she wanted from the builder's collection of plans. They meticulously selected the finishes for both exterior and interior. This was to be Carol's dream home and she wanted it to be hers down to the nails. When she was convinced that the builder and architect had a complete understanding of what she wanted she left Florida.

Her plan was to travel for the summer while the house was built. She spent time in Canada with friends in Toronto. Some weeks she spent in the cottage country of Muskoka. She had an extended stay with her daughter's family in Calgary and enjoyed immensely her new granddaughter. Towards the end of August, a plan was made to fly to Naples to see the progress of her new home. She made an appointment with the builder's representative for the day after she arrived. The next morning, after breakfast she met at his office. After the pleasantries were exchanged the builder indicated that all was going well with the project. The home should be delivered right on time in a month.

"Let's go have a look." Carol said. The builder indicated that he would drive her to the site.

176

Driving up to the lot Carol stared out the passenger side window for a long time. The builder kept up a steady stream of rhetoric about what a wonderful company they were. Finally, Carol turned toward the man in the driver's seat with a troubled look.

"This is NOT my house." She said it with the force of belief.

"Of course, it is." The salesman replied with a big smile. "This is lot number ten on your street. You selected it."

"No, this is not the house that I contracted for. This is the lot that I picked, but this is not my house on it." She said it with the conviction that she knew she was right.

The house was nearly complete. The exterior finishes were done except for the landscaping. Interiors were painted and plumbing ,cabinets and such were in place. It was the wrong house, not the plan she wanted. The garage doors were on the wrong side.

"I'm going in." Carol said as she opened the car door.

"You can't go in there without hard hat and boots" he cried out.

She shot him a stern look as she swung the door shut. Striding through the sand to the front door she walked in. The salesman hurried after her and stood in open doors calling out to her as Carol inspected the interior.

"Let's go back to my office and we'll discuss this." He was getting really nervous now.

After Carol was done with her inspection, they drove in silence back to the office. He pulled her files, and they reviewed the contracts and plans. An ashen look took over his face as he realized that they had built the wrong house on her lot. The builder was now searching for a solution to this problem and the negotiation began. The only thing that he could offer was some free upgraded to the fixtures or the pool. The cost of the house was fixed and there could be no monetary compensation for their mistake.

Carol felt injured as she got up to leave. "I'll give you an answer in the morning," she said. "I'm going to have to think about this." Carol spent the rest of the day trying to resolve the issue in her mind. At the end of the day, she concluded that it "is what it is." The house was almost done, and she would have to accept it. The next morning, she called the builder before she even had coffee. Ready to accept the salesman's offer of some free upgrades, Carol thought that they might get together to work that out today.

"They are tearing that house down as we speak!" The salesman exclaimed.

It was hard to believe but the builder was taking down that nearly built house and was going to honor the contract that Carol had made. She would get her house. Of course, it would be late, and Carol was forced to rent a place to stay. It would be March before the new house was ready and Carol could move in. The house was beautiful, and the pool was spectacular but there were problems. Carol had contracted for marble to surround the master bath; the builder had used ceramic tile. They argued about it for days. The salesman's bonus was dependent on a positive review of ten on a scale of one to ten from the buyer. He asked Carol for a ten rating, Carol told him his rating was two. After his pleading Carol told him that he would get a ten when the master bath was trimmed in marble as she contracted for. In spite of his complaints that they were losing money, the builder put in the marble.

This went on for a year. When the rainy season came that summer the front doors leaked. It was obvious then that the sidewalk was sloping toward the doors. Again, the arguing went on for too long before the builder would fix it. The whole experience was adding to the fact that Carol didn't want to live there any longer. Before two years spent at The Isles, she put the house on the market. When it sold, she was able to take a small profit and buy a luxury condominium on the Gulf Shore. With her determination she hired a contractor, had it gutted to the outside walls and proceeded to rebuild. The new unit was outfitted with all custom cabinets and fixtures and she decorated it to her style. She was there to supervise every step of the construction.

The journey to this time from her beginnings has been a life filled with experiences both positive and not. It took inherent fortitude to overcome the tragic loss that she experienced as a young child. Carol built her comfortable life from no advantages. There was nothing but work to survive in the isolation of the farm in North Ontario. The creativity and effort to build five businesses out of nothing but ideas. The ingenuity to carve out a new career in fundraising and the audacity to succeed beyond the goals established for her.

Today Carol enjoys an idyllic life of winters in the warm sun of Florida and summers on the shore of Lake Ontario looking over the water north to her adored Toronto and beyond.

I have overheard her many times on the phone with a customer service agent somewhere.

"My name is Carol Ethier."

"That's E as in Echo, T as in Tango…"

CAROL ETHIER

My life journey has had many lovely moments as well as a number of 'steep hills and sharp corners'. Life has granted me numerous lifelong friends, for which I am eternally grateful. Lessons have been learned from my countless and varied experiences.

My childhood was challenging and without laughter. I was dedicated to my strong Mother. My sole purpose was to make her life easier while caring for my 'Baby Brother' whom I adore to this day. He is the 'son I never had'.

The many life altering experiences made me who I am. The telling of my stories in an honest and detailed way has granted me a wonderful and welcome peace of mind. I've told my daughter, Mikelle, the therapy she has encouraged me to have for many years has happened. 'E is for Echo' has been and continues to be overwhelmingly cathartic.

It is my sincere wish that this book will inspire those who feel there is no way forward, to keep pushing, to not give up, to look ahead. Convince yourself, in whatever way that works for you, that there is hope.

Above all, I hope that my beloved Daughter & Grandchildren will benefit, however indirectly, from the story of my journey.

Determination and resilience have brought me far. To all who read this book, be strong, be determined, be resilient and search for the positive in all things. I now look back over the years, remember the challenges, quietly celebrate the victories and wish my now blissfully happy life to all.

Kind Regards,

Carol Ethier

CPSIA information can be obtained
at www.ICGtesting.com
Printed in the USA
BVHW051748130721
611837BV00002B/281